CROWN OF
ALEPPO

This book is dedicated in loving memory of

Murad and Sarina Faham

At the risk of their lives, and without reward, they rescued the
Crown of Aleppo
Keter Aram Tsova
and delivered it to Jerusalem and the Jewish people.

From their children
Ben and Marie Dweck
and
their children, grandchildren, and great-grandchildren.

CROWN OF
ALEPPO

THE

MYSTERY

OF THE OLDEST

HEBREW BIBLE

CODEX

Hayim Tawil & Bernard Schneider

2010 • 5770
Philadelphia

JPS is a nonprofit educational association and the oldest and foremost publisher of Judaica in English in North America. The mission of JPS is to enhance Jewish culture by promoting the dissemination of religious and secular works, in the United States and abroad, to all individuals and institutions interested in past and contemporary Jewish life.

The Jewish Publication Society
2100 Arch Street, 2nd floor
Philadelphia, PA 19103
www.jewishpub.org

Design and Composition by Alfred Venditto/Popkitchen

Manufactured in the United States of America

10 11 12   10 9 8 7 6 5 4 3 2 1

Library of Congress Cataloging-in-Publication Data:

The Crown of Aleppo : the mystery of the oldest Hebrew Bible codex /
Hayim Tawil and Bernard Schneider.—1st ed.
p. cm.
Includes bibliographical references and index.
ISBN 978-0-8276-0895-5 (alk. paper)
1. Bible. O.T. Hebrew. Aleppo Codex. 2. Bible. O.T.—Manuscripts, Hebrew. 3. Jews—Syria—Aleppo—History. I. Schneider, Bernard, 1966- II. Aleppo Codex. III. Title.

BS715.5.A43T39 2010

221.4'40956913—dc22

2009038821

**We would like to express our sincere appreciation to Dr. Aaron Feingold
for his ongoing interest in and support for this book.**

JPS books are available at discounts for bulk purchases for reading groups, special sales, and fundraising purchases. Custom editions, including personalized covers, can be created in larger quantities for special needs. For more information, please contact us at marketing@jewishpub.org or at this address: 2100 Arch Street, Philadelphia, PA 19103.

To my parents, Esther and Joseph Tawil (ז"ל)
To my daughter, Taphat Tonia;
To my son, Arye Joseph,
my daughter-in-law, Limor,
my grandson, Hod Hayim,
and my granddaughter, Hadar Ziviah (יבל"א)

*"Grandchildren are the crown of their elders
and the glory of children are their parents."*
PROVERBS 17:6

To my beloved wife, Dr. Josephine Tsakok,
without whose support this book would not have been written.

"An intelligent wife is a gift from God."
PROVERBS 19:14

And to my parents,
Ruth (née Anhang) (ז"ל) and Dr. Samuel Schneider

CONTENTS

Contents

The Bible is, inarguably, the preeminent work of Jewish law, history, and literature. Without it, there would be no Judaism and no Jewish nation, at least not as we know them today. The Bible forms the basis of the Jewish religion and outlines Jewish ethics. It also tells the story of the birth and first two millennia of the Jewish people, documenting the nation's historic presence in and connection to the Land of Israel.

The story of the Crown of Aleppo, also known as the Aleppo Codex, is inextricably linked to the history of the Jewish people. This codex, completed in the 10th century by Tiberian scholars known as Masoretes, sets out the definitive text of the Bible. But perhaps even more important, its very existence reflects the centuries of exile and upheaval, struggle and rebirth that have shaped the Jewish people. Indeed, the Crown of Aleppo, like the Bible itself, contains an important key to understanding Jewish traditions of scholarship and identity.

Through the centuries, the Bible has been passed down by generations of scholars and scribes through the Masorah. The Aleppo Codex represents these scholars' crowning achievement: the most authoritative rendering of the Bible, complete with instructions for reading and singing the text. It was completed ca. 930 C.E. in Tiberias by the scribes Shlomo ben Buya'a and Aharon ben Asher, both scions of prominent scribal families. Ben Buya'a wrote the consonantal text; Ben Asher added the vocalization, accentuation and cantillation marks, which indicate how the text should be read and sung. The codex's significance cannot be overstated, as its writing both provided a definitive, accurate text and assured its transmission for generations.

In the centuries that followed, the codex would trace a tortuous path of loss and redemption, traveling from Jerusalem to Cairo and finally to Aleppo, where it was safeguarded for more than five hundred years. Yet even today, more than 50 years after it was rescued from Aleppo and returned to Israel, the land where it was originally written, this patrimony of the Jewish people is not properly understood or appreciated. We hope this work will go some small way toward remedying this situation. In the chapters that follow, we trace the codex from its inception to the present day, uncovering the stories not only of its journey, but of the journeys of those who came in contact with it.

Unless otherwise indicated or clear from context, and except for certain book and article titles, translations from the Hebrew are those of the authors; in some cases, slight modifications have been made to allow the text to flow smoothly in English.

Hebrew transliteration is based on the 2006 revision of the Guidelines of the Academy of the Hebrew Language, except in quotations, where it conflicts with an accepted spelling or established usage, or where there is an official transliteration of a name or an article, a journal or a book title.

Hayim Tawil
Bernard Schneider

New York, October 2009

This book would not have been possible without the efforts of many individuals, to all of whom we owe a debt of gratitude. We are indebted to the men and women of the following institutions for their courteous assistance. At the Ben-Zvi Institute in Jerusalem: Schlomo Lavi, curator of the photo archive, and especially Michael Glatzer, academic secretary of the Institute, for giving so generously of his time. At Beth Hatefutsoth, Museum of the Jewish Diaspora in Tel Aviv: Zippi Rosenne, director of the Oster Visual Documentation Center, for her unlimited and tireless cooperation in providing the photos of the Great Synagogue. At Hebrew University in Jerusalem: Danna Philosoph-Hovav, coordinator of the photo archive and donor plaques, for her kind help. At the Israel Museum in Jerusalem: Michael Maggen, head of paper conservation, for explaining the conservation of the Crown of Aleppo. At the Jewish Theological Seminary in New York: David Sklar, library specialist in Jewish art and special collections, for his prompt attention to our requests.

Yeshiva University in New York provided us with particular assistance. Our sincerest gratitude to Norman Goldberg, chief photographer, and his assistant, Peter Robertson; Frank Guelpa, Production Department; John Moryl, head librarian, Pollack Library; Mary Ann Linahan, head of interlibrary loans,

Pollack Library; and Zalman Alpert, reference librarian, Gottesman Library. Throughout this project, our research was greatly aided by the professionalism extended to us by Zvi Erenyi, acquisitions librarian, Gottesman Library. Special thanks also to Dr. Hillel Davis, vice president for university life, and Dr. Morton Lowengrub, provost.

We are indebted to Michail Kizilov for supplying us with a rare photo of the Firkovich family, which he found in the Department of Manuscripts of the library of the Lithuanian Academy of Sciences. Special thanks are due to Harry Epstein, Sruli Rapps, and Yossi Bilig for their generous assistance. We are grateful to Abraham Peer, Moses Faham, and Joseph Faham for providing us with important photos and documents concerning their father, Murad (Mordechai) Faham. We also owe a debt of gratitude to our colleagues Professor Samuel Schneider and Professor Richard White for their scholarly suggestions. Our thanks go to Gloria Silbert for her dedicated work in collecting and organizing the photographs.

Last but not least, we are grateful to our editors at the Jewish Publication Society. In particular, we would like to thank Mindy Brown, for her exceptional editorial work, and managing editor, Janet L. Liss, for her guidance and suggestions. We would also especially like to thank Dr. Ellen Frankel, editor emeritas, for her consistent encouragement. Without her vision and determination this book would not have come to fruition.

Needless to say, any errors are the responsibility of the authors.

CROWN OF
ALEPPO

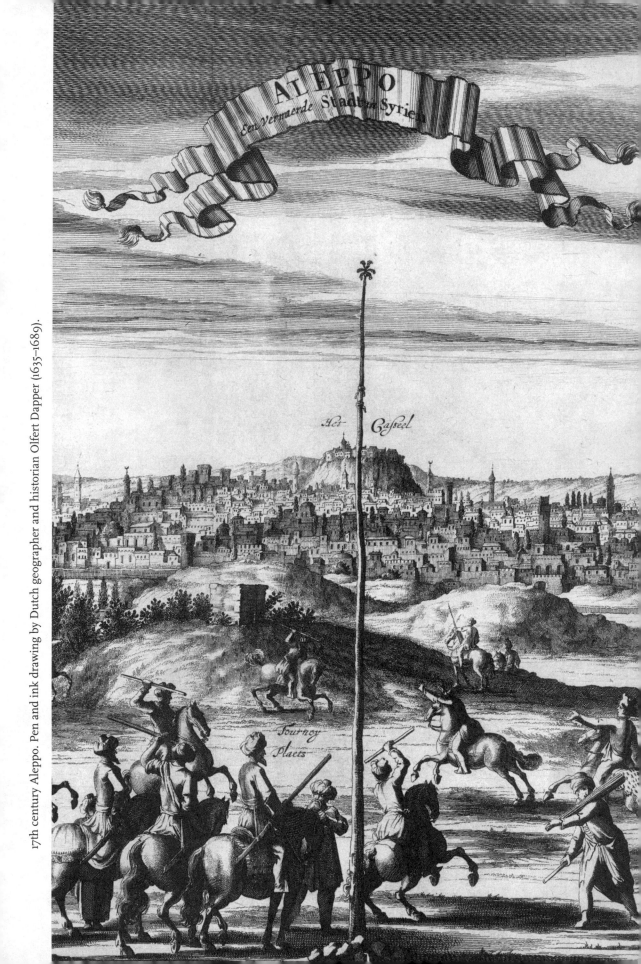

17th century Aleppo. Pen and ink drawing by Dutch geographer and historian Olfert Dapper (1635–1689).

1

THE CATASTROPHE OF 1947

Thirty miles south of the Syrian–Turkish border and halfway between the Euphrates River and the Mediterranean Sea, a city rises up from the bleak landscape. Thousands of shops, homes, bazaars, and covered markets constructed out of limestone line the city's streets, and the skyline is punctuated by minarets that climb toward heaven from numerous mosques. Many of the mosques and homes within the city have turned gray with age; thus the city, whose name derives from the word "white" or "milk," has become known as *"Haleb ash-Shahba,"* or "Aleppo the Gray." Aleppo is one of the oldest continuously inhabited cities in the world. Archaeologists have unearthed cuneiform tablets at the ancient Syrian settlement of Mari dating from the 18th century B.C.E. which mention Aleppo by name,[1] but the city may well have been founded even earlier. Aleppo reached its zenith under Ottoman rule, when it served as an administrative center for the surrounding provinces. It was even more important as a trading town because it was a vital stop for merchants traveling between Asia and Europe.

Crowning the highest hill of the city is the Citadel of Aleppo, considered by many to be the most impressive medieval fortress in the Middle East. Built by Saladin's son al-Zahir al-Ghazi in 1209, on top of ruins dating to the Greek and Roman periods, the citadel was damaged by a Mamluk attack in 1400 before being refortified by the Ottomans in the 16th century. Even today, the citadel is visible from almost any point in the city and serves as a reminder of the region's great historical past and of an age when Aleppo was world renown.

According to Aleppan Jewish tradition, Jews first arrived in Aleppo after King David conquered the region in the 10th century B.C.E. For hundreds of years, the city certainly saw Jewish traders, and Jews made their home there; however, scholars date the founding of the city's Jewish community to not later than the Roman period.[2] As People of the Book (*'Ahl al-Kitāb*), the Jews of Aleppo, like those in other Muslim lands, were considered *dhimmi*, permanent second-class citizens under the "protection" of the Muslim state. *Dhimmi* were prohibited from owning arms and from building or restoring synagogues. They were subject to special taxes and penal laws (for example, *dhimmi* were not allowed to testify in court) and were required to wear special clothing. In general, they lived under the constant threat of abasement and humiliation.[3] Despite their precarious position, however, Aleppo's Jews managed to live relatively undisturbed next to their Muslim neighbors until the middle of the 20th century. The partition of the Land of Israel would mark the final turning point in the history of Aleppo's Jewish community.

In retrospect, ominous clouds had begun to gather over Aleppo years before Israel's partition, with the first indications of trouble appearing at the end of World War I. In 1932, Anṭūn Saʿādah (1904–1949), a Greek Orthodox Lebanese who was an admirer of Hitler and deeply influenced by fascist ideology, founded the fascist Syrian Social Nationalist Party. Both the name of the party and its insignia, a modified reverse swastika, were clearly inspired by the German Nazi party. The party's anthem was even sung to the tune of *"Deutschland über alles."* Saʿādah called for the establishment of a totalitarian state and for a Greater Syrian nationalism that hearkened back to a pre-Islamic past. Saʿādah's vision included everyone but the Jews, Zionist or not.[4]

By the 1930s, there were also Syrian Steel Shirts, modeled after the German Brown Shirts, who wore steel gray shirts and trousers, and black ties, belts, and

The Citadel of Aleppo, shown in two photos from ca. 1947, was a medieval fortified palace whose remains still stand at the center of the old city of Aleppo. The citadel is believed to be one of the oldest and one of the largest castles in the world.

sidara caps. Their insignia was a hand bearing a torch; their salute resembled the German *heil*. Although the Steel Shirts numbered only in the thousands, they were highly visible in Syria.[5] Their activities had a considerable chilling effect on the country's Jews.

Thus in the years after World War I, and especially by the 1930s, the Jews of Aleppo began to realize that the long period of relative peace in the city was coming to an end. Thousands left Syria for the Americas in the interwar years.

Anti-Jewish activity increased in the run-up to Syrian independence and in reaction to increasing tensions between Arabs and Jews in Israel. After Syria negotiated its independence from France in 1936 (although full independence was deferred until 1946), the new Syrian government issued directives against the Jews, restricting their movement, denying them the right to leave the country, and requiring them to carry papers indicating their religion.[6] Tensions between the Jews and Muslims continued to increase in Syria, as they did throughout the Arab world, in part because of Arab anger over the return of Jews to Israel.

In July 1937, the Palestine Royal Commission, better known as the Peel Commission, proposed that the Land of Israel be partitioned into two states — one Jewish and one Arab — the latter of which might then be merged into Transjordan.[7] The Jews accepted the British plan with misgivings; the Arabs vehemently opposed it, rejecting it the day after it was issued. By late 1947, Arab anger over the plan had reached a boiling point. The Arab countries threatened to move their forces into Israel and decimate the Jewish population if the United Nations voted in favor of partition. Arab spokesmen at the United Nations also warned they would not be able to protect their native Jewish populations from mob attack if partition was approved.[8]

By the time the UN vote was finally taken on November 29, 1947, it was late afternoon in New York City. Although it was already nighttime in the Middle East, many people there remained awake to hear the results. When the final tally came in — 33 to 13, with 10 abstentions, in favor of partition and the reestablishment of Jewish sovereignty[9] — celebrations began in Israel. People clogged Tel Aviv's streets, while David Ben-Gurion and Golda Myerson (later Meir) addressed cheering crowds from the balcony of the Jewish Agency in

Jerusalem.[10] The Ashkenazi chief rabbi of Israel, Isaac Herzog, emotionally declared, "After a darkness of two thousand years, the dawn of redemption has broken."[11] Jews around the world applauded the decision, which paved the way for the creation of the modern State of Israel. For Jews elsewhere in the Middle East, however, the vote was cause for fear as well as joy.

Aleppo in 1947 had two principal Jewish neighborhoods. The wealthier Jamiliya community, in the west of the city, was built at the turn of the century and showed the influence of Western architecture. Middle-class Jews and Arabs made their homes there. The old Jewish quarter, the *Harat al-Yahud,* where the poorer Jews lived, was in Bahsita, the old city. Most of the gray stone houses along the small, cramped alleyways had been constructed at the beginning of the Ottoman period and were generally in disrepair. Near the entrance to the quarter was al-Kitab, the Jewish primary school, with its bare walls and shaky desks.[12]

The pogrom in Aleppo began on Sunday, November 30. The Arabs demanded that the Jews close their shops and stay at home. The Jewish community had no choice but to comply. The next day, the Syrian army gathered in the Jewish quarter; the largest contingent of soldiers was found at the Great Synagogue, allegedly to protect it from throngs of angry Arabs. Two leaders of the Jewish community, Siahu Shamah and Rahmo Nehmad, spoke to Aleppo's governor, who guaranteed the safety of the Jewish community. Shamah did not believe that the governor would stop the mobs, but Nehmad was more optimistic.[13]

By noon, a frenzied Arab mob filled the square in front of the Great Synagogue and spilled out into the side streets, chanting, *"Falestin beladna, we al Yehud kalabna,"* or "Palestine is ours, and the Jews are our dogs."[14] The Arab citizens then stormed the synagogue and, with the soldiers' help, ransacked and burned it. Smaller groups advanced through the Jewish quarter, continuing their ugly chant, while the Jews shut themselves in their homes and prayed. The army remained on the sidelines as the mob burned synagogues and schools, and they kept the Jews off the streets so that the angry rabble could plunder and wreck the quarter until late into the night. Only after the damage had been done did the army disperse the mob. The next day, according to one eyewitness account, the chief of police inspected the ruins and smiled.[15]

A few days later, Shamah, Nehmad, and Rabbi Moshe Tawil, the chief rabbi of Aleppo, went to see the Syrian president, Shukri al-Quwatli. Al-Quwatli expressed regret over what had happened but claimed he was unaware of the riot. He expressed disbelief that such a thing could occur in Aleppo, but refused to take any action in response, stating, "Whatever was done is done." After this meeting, the Syrian Jews asked the president to safeguard their community in the future.[16] By then, of course, it was too late; most of the important buildings and much personal property had already been destroyed, as the authorities had no doubt intended.

Murad Faham, a Jewish cheese merchant in Aleppo who was present during the pogrom, provided eyewitness testimony about the events surrounding the pogrom. He recalled that once the plan to partition the Land of Israel began to move forward, the situation for the Jews of Aleppo worsened considerably. In addition to the legal restrictions imposed on them, unofficial discrimination against Syria's Jews also increased. Jewish merchants were threatened, and young women were harassed in the street. Many of the more affluent Jews started to leave Aleppo, which further weakened the position of the Jews who remained behind. The day after the United Nations vote, Faham was on his way to the market when he ran into Siahu Shamah, who asked Faham to tell the Jewish shopkeepers to close their businesses. When Faham, unaware of the political situation, asked why, Shamah whispered that there were rumors of impending trouble. Faham did as requested. On his way home, he ran into Mansour Gilingi, an Arab acquaintance, who urged him to return home quickly. When Faham saw schoolchildren demonstrating against the partition plan, he grew frightened. But when some of his Bedouin business partners wanted to take him and his family to the safety of their encampment outside the city, Faham chose to remain with the Jewish community. He fortified the doors of his house and moved his family to the kitchen, which had windows looking onto the alley, so his sons could see what was going on outside without being seen by the mobs. Faham also gave shelter to 43 Jewish children from the neighborhood.[17]

Because he had been told that the government had mobilized smiths and other craftsmen to help destroy the Jewish quarter, Faham was certain his home defenses would eventually be breached. He knew that he had to evacuate his

The outdoor *tevah* (pulpit) and Summer Courtyard of the Great Synagogue (ca. 1978), after its destruction in the pogrom of 1947. (*Courtesy of Beth Hatefutsoth, Photo Archive, Tel Aviv.*)

9

pregnant wife and six children (three boys and three girls) along with the 43 children who had been placed in his care. Climbing up to his roof, he saw his neighbor Rabbi Tawil, who asked him to recite *Tehillim* (Psalms) before leaving home. Faham brought his household and the neighborhood children to the roof and started to look for an escape route.

It was then that Faham heard a man call his name. Not recognizing the voice, Faham feared a trick. When he asked who was calling, the voice replied, "Don't you recognize me? We grew up together. I am the cousin of Hamdu Rajab, the merchant in Bab Jenin who buys all his cheese from you." Faham helped his family and the other children climb from rooftop to rooftop until they reached Rajab's home nearby. For several days they remained hidden, in time learning of the destruction of Bahsita, the Jewish areas of Jamaliya, and Jewish-owned shops throughout Aleppo.[18]

In an interview nearly three decades later, Faham recalled:

> I asked [an Arab who was protecting me], "What about the Great Synagogue?" He answered me, "They burned it. You don't have even one book left. Not in the school, not in the synagogue. All were burned." I asked him, "How were [the books] in the iron safe burned?" He told me that the government, instead of equipping the fire engines with water, had equipped them with benzene, which had burned everything, even the books inside the iron safe. I asked, "What are they doing now?" He answered, "The government has sent cavalry from the army, to take a census of which houses and stores belonged to Jews and which to non-Jews."[19]

The pogrom took a heavy toll on the Jewish community of Aleppo. Tens were killed and scores injured during the riot.[20] In addition, the most important structures in the community—the Great Synagogue, several other synagogues, and schools—were ravaged by fire.

For many days after the pogrom, the Jews of Aleppo were afraid to leave their homes. A few courageous individuals ventured out at different times to see if they could salvage some of the precious items from the Great Synagogue, which was still smoldering. When they entered the building, they were horrified by what they found. The glittering crystal chandeliers were smashed, the golden menorahs and the silver adornments for the Torah crowns were

Exterior model of the Great Synagogue of Aleppo shows how the synagogue is believed to have looked prior to its destruction in the pogrom of 1947. The old Western Wing appears on the far right of the model and the new Eastern Wing and small courtyard are on the left. (*Courtesy of Beth Hatefutsoth, Photo Archive, Tel Aviv.*)

A model of the outdoor courtyard and *tevah* of the Great Synagogue. The ornate dome of the actual structure (shown in the photo on page 14) does not appear in this model. (*Courtesy of Beth Hatefutsoth, Photo Archive, Tel Aviv.*)

The ruins of the Great Synagogue of Aleppo in two photos from 1979. (*Courtesy of Beth Hatefutsoth, Photo Archive, Tel Aviv.*)

missing, the ornamental curtains of the arks were in shreds, and burned fragments of Torah scrolls were scattered on the floor.

The Jewish community was shattered by the pogrom. It has been estimated that immediately before the pogrom there were 10,000 Jews in Aleppo. Only a few months later, more than half the inhabitants had fled, and the population continued to decline thereafter. Because Jews required permission to leave the city, which generally was not granted, most were forced to escape under cover of darkness.[21] Those who did not leave Aleppo found themselves living in increasingly poor conditions. The situation deteriorated further after the Six-Day War in 1967. It was not until the 1990s that Syrian president Hafez al-Assad allowed the last Syrian Jews to leave the country.[22] Today, no Jews are known to be living in Aleppo.

For centuries, the greatest treasure of the Aleppo community was a codex, an early form of leaved book of the Hebrew Bible[23] known as the Aleppo Codex, or the Crown of Aleppo, from its Hebrew name *Keter Aram Tsova*. Written by the scribe Shlomo ben Buya'a in the early 10th century c.e., it was vocalized by Aharon ben Asher, the last and most important member of the Ben Asher family of Masoretic scribes.[24] The codex, which had been in Aleppo since at least the 15th century, was the oldest known complete text of the Bible and was unsurpassed for its accuracy and faithfulness to the Masorah. It was also the most reliable source for Hebrew vocalization, making it one of the most important documents in Jewish history.

What happened to the Crown during the 1947 pogrom? About one month after the pogrom, an article in the Israeli newspaper *Haaretz* appeared, explaining the value of the Crown and lamenting its unfortunate loss in the fire that destroyed the Great Synagogue of Aleppo. "If what the newspapers have said turns out to be correct," the author of the article wrote, "the renowned Bible that was the splendor of the Jewish community of Aleppo, a Bible that according to tradition Maimonides himself used, has been consumed by fire in the pogrom against the Jews that broke out a few weeks ago. The *Keter Aram Tsova*, as it was accustomed to be called, is lost forever."[25]

13

Outdoor *tevah* (pulpit) in the Summer Courtyard of the Great Synagogue of Aleppo, prior to its destruction in 1947. (*Courtesy of Beth Hatefutsoth, Photo Archive, Jerusalem.*)

2

ORIGINS OF THE CROWN
AND ITS SIGNIFICANCE

Before we can properly appreciate the particular features that made the Crown of Aleppo such an important volume, we must trace the history of the codex form and the Tiberian Masoretic tradition.

Development of the Codex

The codex, invented by the Romans in the 1st century C.E., represented a technological advancement over its predecessors—the clay tablet and the parchment or papyrus scroll. Consisting of handwritten manuscript leaves secured between hard covers, the codex marked a transition between two forms of publication. This new book format possessed two important advantages over the scroll: it was more portable and, significantly, more accessible. Like recordings on the now outmoded audiotape, the information stored in a scroll is only accessible through a linear reading. To read what is at the end of a scroll, a reader has no choice but to unfurl the entire scroll. By contrast, a codex—that is, a leaved book—is like a CD or DVD, which provides access to all information directly, no matter where such information is stored on the disk. Books are also cheaper to produce because the text can be written or printed on both sides of the page, whereas scrolls are written or printed on only one side.

Because of these significant advantages, codices caught on quickly and were in common use by the 4th century c.e.[1] Although Hebrew texts may have first taken codex form during this time, the first documented evidence that Jews were using codices dates from the 8th century c.e.[2] The earliest surviving copies of Hebrew codices, primarily biblical texts, date to the 10th century.[3]

To understand the significant role played by the codex in the history of the Hebrew Bible, it is important to recall how the Bible was transmitted before the codex was invented. Until about the 10th century c.e., the Bible was hand-written by scribes in scroll form. The oldest and most famous biblical scrolls, dating to the late Second Temple period, are part of the collection known as the Dead Sea Scrolls. Similar scroll libraries would have been found in the Temple precincts and the royal quarters in Jerusalem as well, although none of these has survived.

Despite the eventual replacement of such parchment scrolls by codices and then by printed books, Judaism never completely abandoned the scroll. To this day, synagogues use scroll versions of the Torah—unvocalized, uncantillated and consisting solely of the twenty-two letters of the Hebrew alphabet with spaces to separate words—for public recitation. In fact, Jewish law requires that only scrolls without any notations—vowels, cantillation marks, or punctuation—may be used in liturgical services in the synagogue. However, these strictures do not apply to the nonliturgical use of the Bible. Accordingly, the Masoretes, a guild of highly trained scribes living in Israel in the 8th to 9th and 10th centuries, turned to the codex form when they wanted to add textual information not permitted on a liturgical scroll. It was this innovation that ultimately allowed for the creation and diffusion of many features we now associate with the biblical text: the punctuation, vocalization, and cantillation marks that aid reading and interpretation, as well as the many commentaries printed alongside the biblical text. Thus, without the codex, much of our knowledge of the Hebrew Bible would have been irretrievably lost.

Tiberias

Between 14 and 18 c.e., Herod Antipas built an administrative city on the remains of the ancient city of Rakat, on the western shore of the Sea of Galilee, and named it after his Roman benefactor, the emperor Tiberius. Although the town was originally shunned by Jews because tombs had been discovered during its construction,[4] because of its proximity to the Sea of Galilee and its hot baths, Tiberias developed into a thriving city. It was a religious center known for its outstanding scholars and many synagogues, and its importance increased after Jews were barred from entering Jerusalem by the emperor Hadrian. In fact, until Jews were allowed to return to Jerusalem after the Muslim conquest in the 7th century c.e., Tiberias functioned as the Jewish capital. Many *tanaim* (the rabbinic sages who composed the Mishnah) lived there, including Rabbi Yose the Galilean, and the *amoraim* Rabbi Yohanan and Reish Lakish. From 235 c.e., it was the seat of the Sanhedrin, and the Jerusalem Talmud was largely composed there.[5]

The local economy was based on fishing and on a variety of cottage industries, such as glass and pottery making, mat and wool weaving, woodworking, and fish farming.[6] Sugarcane was grown in the region and the remains of ancient sugar mills have been found. After the serendipitous capture of several Chinese craftsmen by Muslim warriors in the 8th century, papermaking, which had been invented in China in the 2nd century c.e., was introduced to the Islamic world;[7] Tiberias soon became one of the centers of the new papermaking and paper-exporting industry. Despite the availability of this new writing material, however, scribes continued to produce Hebrew Bibles, whether in scroll or codex, the old-fashioned way — on parchment.[8]

Until the Crusaders' conquest of 1099, Israel served as the center of the Hebrew language for Jews throughout the Diaspora. Given Tiberias's well-established scholarly and scribal communities and its thriving papermaking industry, it is not surprising that the city was a major producer of Hebrew-language books for the Jewish world. Its craftsmen produced holy, semi-holy (*agada* and *piyut*), and secular books. It was also known for the publication of Hebrew translations of Arabic works, which were thus made accessible to Jewish scholars throughout the world. (Rashi, for example, consulted a copy of *Sefer haNikud,* a grammar book written by Saadia Gaon that had been translated from Arabic to Hebrew in Tiberias.)[9]

In the early 12th century, the city was destroyed by the Crusaders, and it remained largely devoid of Jews until the 16th century.[10] Benjamin of Tudela, the famous Jewish traveler, reports that in 1170, there were only 50 Jews in Tiberias.[11]

Ultimately, in the centuries before the city's destruction, Tiberias's Hebrew book-producing industry had undergone three major innovations. The first two were the shifts from handwritten scrolls to handwritten books, and from parchment to paper. (Printed Hebrew books, of course, came much later. The first known printing of a Hebrew book, an edition of Rashi's commentaries, occurred in 1475 in the Italian city of Regio de Calabria.)[12] The third major change was the perfection of the Tiberian notational system.[13]

The Development of Notational Systems and the Advent of the Tiberian Masoretes

Hebrew, like certain other Semitic languages including Phoenician and Aramaic, does not use letters to represent vowels; letters represent only consonants. Pronunciation can, therefore, be difficult to determine, particularly in the case of homographs, of which there are many in Hebrew. For example, the Hebrew letters *"dalet-bet-resh,"* when unvocalized, can denote the noun "word" or "statement" (*davar*); a form of the verb "to speak" (*daber*), derived from the same root as the noun; or the word "pestilence" (*dever*), among other possibilities. To complicate matters further, ancient written Hebrew did not include punctuation. Up to that point, ancient scrolls, like the Dead Sea Scrolls, marked divisions between words but not between phrases, sentences, chapters, or weekly readings. Furthermore, there were also no markings in the text to indicate vocalization, punctuation, or cantillation. Accordingly, the correct understanding and pronunciation of the Bible originally depended solely on the strength of the oral tradition.

By the period of the Dead Sea Scrolls (ca. 250 B.C.E. – 100 C.E.), scribes had developed various strategies to guide readers in the pronunciation and interpretation of biblical texts. They designated four letters of the Hebrew alphabet — *"aleph,"* "he," "vav," and "yud" (the *imot hakriya* or *matres lectionis;* literally, "mothers of reading") — to indicate vowel sounds. However, many scribes failed to add these "vowels" regularly or consistently.

The early scribes also invented a form of shorthand notation called *serugin,* which they sometimes used for nonliturgical biblical texts. Manuscripts written in this form would include only the first word of every verse; important words or words likely to cause confusion were indicated by including one or more letters as well as accentuation or vowel signs as mnemonic devices.[14] Such texts are referred to in the Talmud.[15]

Clearly, these kinds of scribal annotations would make sense only when used in conjunction with a copy of the unvocalized biblical text (that is, a scroll meant for liturgical use) and would be of interest only to educated readers who knew the text by heart but could benefit from a few reminders. As the oral tradition weakened and the general level of learning declined, more notations were needed — and added.[16]

Three major notation systems were developed, roughly simultaneously, in Babylonia, Tiberias, and elsewhere in Israel (especially in the south); accordingly, they are generally referred to as the Babylonian, Tiberian, and Land of Israel systems. It is not known precisely when these notation systems originated; however, a full-fledged Tiberian system emerged by the 10th century C.E. Based on what we know about the development of graphic notation systems, we can take an educated guess that it took about 200 years for the Tiberian system to develop. This suggests that the earliest systematic attempts began in about 700 C.E.

What triggered the need for such notation systems at this particular time?

One possibility is that the Arab conquest of the Land of Israel in the early 7th century put the Hebrew language at risk. Once the political situation had calmed, Jewish scholars set to work devising a method to establish the correct reading of the Bible and the correct pronunciation of the Hebrew language that could be used by future generations.[17] However, since Aramaic had already supplanted Hebrew as the language of daily use, it is difficult to believe that Arabic posed much of a threat to Hebrew, which was by this time mostly a literary language.

A more likely impetus spurring the development of the biblical notation system was the rise of the Karaites, a group of Jews who emphasized the primacy of the Bible over rabbinic literature and thus were particularly concerned with ascertaining the correct biblical text. Their conflict with the Rabbanites over a range of halakhic issues demanded a close reading and precise interpretation of the Bible. This communal quarrel led to a flowering of work on the biblical text and greater attention to the Hebrew language more generally.

Of the three main notation systems developed during this period, the Tiberian was the most sophisticated and complete and, as far as is known, the last to develop. It was a comprehensive system that not only conveyed the parsing of the verse (that is, punctuation) and the melody for liturgical reading, as did the earlier two systems, but also marked the stress within words. The Tiberian system, too, had the most developed system for vocalization.[18] By contrast, for example, the Land of Israel system noted only the five cardinal vowels; further, their usage was not consistent, with several vowel signs sometimes used interchangeably.[19]

The Tiberian system perfected by the city's Masoretes remedied the declining level of knowledge of the Hebrew language in several ways. It allowed the Masoretes to fix these oral traditions in written form. They made final determinations regarding all aspects of the text and codified their decisions in their notational system.

These scholars established the spelling of every single word in the Bible, determining whether a word should be written "full" (*ktiv male*) or "defective" *(ktiv haser)* — that is, with or without *imot hakriya* (the four "vowel letters"). They also introduced vocalization and accentuation marks (the *nekudot,* or diacritical marks). These notations were vital for ensuring the transmission of the correct pronunciation. Without them, the reader requires knowledge of the oral tradition in order to pronounce words correctly. For example, a common sequence of letters in the Bible is *"vav-yud-alef-mem-resh,"* which can be read *"vayomer," or "vayomar,"* both variations of "and he said," but with differing vocalization, or *"veyomar,"* which means "let him say." In many cases, neither context nor grammar rules offer the reader any help and the reader's only recourse is the oral tradition.

The Masoretes also inserted cantillation marks (*taamim* or *taame hamikra*) into the text. These marks indicate the correct melody for chanting the text out loud in the synagogue. But they provide much more than musical information; they also convey aspects of punctuation; indicate the accented syllable; designate the middle and end of each verse (something that is not always clear from the text itself); specify the conjunction or disjunction of words, thus indicating phrases; and often convey the narrative drama.[20] In these ways, the cantillation marks provide us with the biblical Hebrew equivalent of commas, semicolons, periods, and sometimes even stage directions.

The Tiberian system's comprehensiveness, and its ultimate inclusion in Aharon ben Moshe ben Asher's 10th-century book *Dikduke haTaamim* (*A Grammar of Cantillation*), a Masoretic treatise that deals with cantillation marks, the vocalization of certain occurrences, and the ways of noting the *shva*,[21] meant that the Tiberian punctuation system became the standard for the vocalized biblical text, and it is still used today in a somewhat modified form. Soon after the system became the standard, it was adopted by different Jewish communities to preserve their own distinct manners of pronunciation. Today, the Tiberian system is used to represent all the ways Hebrew is spoken, from modern Israeli to Yemenite to Polish to *Mizrahi* (certain Jewish communities from the Middle East). Thus, although the writing of this notational system has not changed much in 1,000 years, the sounds it signifies today now bear only limited resemblance to the Tiberian pronunciation for which the system was originally designed.[22]

The system that describes the biblical text as annotated by the Tiberian Masoretes is known as the Masorah, which means "that which is handed down or transmitted." There is not, however, a single authoritative Masorah text. Once the fully marked and vocalized text of the Bible was finally established, each Masorete made notes on his copy of the text, which were included in his codices. Individual Masoretes decided which annotations to include; therefore, no two manuscripts are exactly the same in this regard.[23] It is important to note, however, that differences between the most faithful representations of the Masorah are fairly minor.

The Masorah — in this case, the Masoretic notes pertaining to specific biblical passages—is divided into two types: the Small Masorah (*Masorah Ketana* or *Masorah Parva*) and the Large Masorah (*Masorah Gedola* or *Masorah Magna*). Notes belonging to the category of the Small Masorah appear in the margins alongside the column or columns of text to which they pertain, with the relevant portion within the text itself marked with a small circle. The abbreviated note in the margin indicates something about the word identified in the text—for example, the letter *"lamed,"* standing for the Aramaic word *"leta,"* or "none," tells us that this word, or this form of the word, appears nowhere else in the Bible. The Small Masorah also indicates whether a particular word is written full or defective; most of the notes in the Small Masorah category are of this latter type.[24]

The notes belonging to the category of the Large Masorah are generally (and in the Crown, always) written at the top or bottom of the page. Their primary purpose is to elaborate on the references noted in the Small Masorah. It is often difficult to decipher comments in the Large Masorah, because they lack references to the chapter divisions and verse numbering with which we are now so familiar. (The chapter and verse divisions were invented by Christian scholars in the Middle Ages, as were the artificial divisions of Samuel, Kings, and Chronicles, and subsequently popularized by printers.[25] These artificial divisions often contradict Jewish tradition, the "open" and "closed" lines of the Masorah, and even the obvious meaning and flow of the text.) In the absence of such a system of fixed citation points, the Large Masorah indentifies relevant verses by referring to other words in those verses or to some other indicator designed to make the reference clear. It also notes words that one might otherwise spell incorrectly as well as full versus defective spellings.[26]

The development of this sophisticated and ingenious system for annotating the Hebrew Bible was the sine qua non for the writing of the Crown of Aleppo, which, along with the Dead Sea Scrolls, is the most important biblical manuscript in Jewish history. Fittingly, the Crown was composed by scions of two of the most prominent dynasties of Tiberian Masoretes: the Ben Asher and Ben Buya'a families.

The Writing of the Crown

In the days before mechanical printing, copying books was an important skill, even an art. Literacy was fairly uncommon and skilled scribes were rare. To be considered competent, a scribe needed good penmanship, artistic skill, and a keen eye for details. Furthermore, the level of care required for copying out the Bible was especially high. (Today, it takes about a year for a scribe to write a Torah scroll; since scribal methods have not changed much in 1,000 years, it is safe to assume that the work of the medieval scribes in Tiberas took as long.)

Handwritten codices of the Torah took a similar amount of time. Based on the colophons of certain Samaritan codices, we know that it took one particular scribe eight years to write thirteen codices. It is not surprising, then, that aspiring scribes began their training at a young age. In 10th-century Tiberias, the center of the Hebrew and Jewish book worlds, many local families were in the scribal business. Students would generally apprentice with one of the three main schools: the Beit Midrash of Saïd ben Pargoi and his star pupil, Shlomo Halevi ben Buya'a; the Beit Midrash of the Ben Ashers; or the Beit Midrash of the Ben Naftalis.[27]

According to traditional attributions, the Aleppo Codex was compiled by members of two of these schools: Aharon ben Asher and Shlomo ben Buya'a. It is believed that Ben Buya'a wrote the unmarked text and Ben Asher added the notations. But who were these men?

Not much is known about either. We know that Aharon ben Asher was the son of Moshe ben Asher ("Ben Asher" being used as the equivalent of today's surnames), a great Masorete in his own right, who wrote a highly regarded codex of the Prophets. Moshe was the fourth-generation scion of a Masoretic dynasty begun by a man named Asher, whose son and grandson, Nehemia ben Asher and Asher ben Nehemia, also carried on the founder's traditions. We know that Ben Buya'a studied the Bible with the Masorete Saïd ben Pargoi,[28] who was undoubtedly known to and perhaps even a good friend of Moshe ben Asher. As prominent scribes, Shlomo ben Buya'a and Aharon ben Asher would likely have frequented the same circles.

23

We know that both Moshe ben Asher and Saïd ben Pargoi aspired to write definitive Masoretic texts, but without their manuscripts, it is impossible to know the extent of their work. The single codex of Moshe ben Asher still extant is that of the Prophets;[29] only a fragment of Saïd ben Pargoi's colophon has survived. It seems likely that each man encouraged his son and pupil, respectively, to undertake a comprehensive codex of the entire Bible. Either at their elders' suggestions, or simply because of the difficulty of the work, Aharon ben Asher and Shlomo ben Buya'a decided to divide the work between them. Ben Buya'a wrote the unmarked text, and Ben Asher focused on completing a perfect copy of the Masorah.

In general, scribes, particularly those writing out the Bible, had an unenviable task. They spent hours transcribing the text, without any opportunity to be creative. Virtually every aspect of writing a Torah scroll is strictly prescribed by Jewish law; scribes adhered to the same constraints when writing a Bible in book form. Furthermore, whereas the biblical text was revered, the scribe remained anonymous.

One of the few places where the scribe could express his individuality was in the colophon. The colophon (from the Greek for "summit" or "finishing touch") refers to the inscription at the end of a manuscript. There and there alone could the scribe add a personal note, stating his name and any other information he wished to include, typically concerning the writing of the scroll or codex. It is the colophon that gives us a small window into the scribe's mind.

Unfortunately, there is no known colophon to the Crown.[30] The page that is often incorrectly referred to as the Crown's colophon was in fact written a little more than a century after the codex was completed; it should be regarded more accurately as a dedication, written to commemorate the Crown's presentation to the Karaite community of Jerusalem in around 1050.[31] Regrettably, even this dedication was lost, along with nearly 200 other pages of the Crown, during the 1947 pogrom in Aleppo. Although several transcriptions of the dedication exist, they are not identical to each other. Probably the most reliable copy is the one found in a 1933 pamphlet by Rabbi Meir Nehmad,[32] a prominent rabbi in Aleppo who claimed to have copied the dedication directly from the codex.[33]

The dedication, as transcribed by Nehmad, begins:

> *This is the complete codex of the twenty-four books [of the Bible], written by the master and teacher Shlomo ben Buya'a the ready [deft] scribe, may God's spirit give him rest, and punctuated and given Masora'h notes by the great teacher and wise sage, master of scribes and father of wise men, head of the teachers, quick of deed and understanding in action, and unique in his generation, the master, Rabbi Aharon son of the master Rabbi Asher, may his soul be bound up in the bonds of life together with the prophets, the righteous and the pious.[34]*

Debates over the Crown have focused on three major questions: (1) Was the Crown indeed written by Ben Buya'a and notated by Ben Asher, making it as old as the dedication and tradition claim? (2) Was the Crown of Aleppo the codex consulted by Maimonides? (3) Were Ben Asher and Ben Buya'a Rabbanites or, as some have claimed, Karaites?

Determining the Crown's Authorship

The question of the authorship and therefore the dating of the Crown was once hotly debated. The esteemed German biblical scholars Heinrich Grätz[35] and Paul Kahle[36] both accepted the tradition of the Aleppan Jews that the Crown was written by Ben Asher and Ben Buya'a, whereas the British scholar William Wickes[37] did not. However, none of these researchers had the opportunity to see the Crown firsthand, relying instead on some photographed pages and transcriptions of the dedication.[38] The Aleppan community that controlled the Crown from 1479 until 1957 restricted access by outside scholars, who were thus forced to rely on secondary sources. Now that scholars have had the opportunity to examine the Crown closely and have access to a wide range of other codices and Hebrew manuscripts, they have concluded that the Crown was indeed written by Ben Buya'a and Ben Asher in the early 10th century. The attribution of the writers and date of the Crown in the dedication is corroborated by external and textual evidence.

The most compelling proof of Ben Buya'a's involvement in writing the Crown derives from a manuscript in the Russian National Library known to have been written by Ben Buya'a. The manuscript was found in Čūfut-Kale, a town in

The Cave of Elijah the Prophet in the Great Synagogue. The Crown of Aleppo was kept in an iron safe in this room. In the center of the photo is a stone structure with an iron fence around it upon which candles were placed. (*Courtesy of Beth Hatefutsoth, Photo Archive, Tel Aviv.*)

Crimea. According to its colophon, the document was written by Shlomo ben Buya'a, notated by his relative Ephraim ben Buya'a, and completed in 930 c.e. When we compare the Crown with this manuscript, it is clear that the two are indeed the product of the same hand.[39] If one assumes that it took several years each to complete the writing of the text and the notations, then the Čūfut-Kale codex was probably started around the middle of the 920s, perhaps as early as the first half of that decade. We can estimate that the Crown was completed around the same time, if not earlier.[40]

Attribution of the Crown's annotation to Aharon Ben Asher has also been carefully analyzed. Scholars look to Mishael Ben Uziel's *Kitab al-Khilaf* (in Hebrew, *Sefer haHilufim*, or *Book of Differences*), produced in the 11th century, which set out more than 1,200 biblical passages where Ben Asher and his Masorete rival, David ben Naftali, disagreed over vocalization, accentuation, and the like. By employing Ben Uziel's close analysis of Ben Asher's approach, researchers discovered his characteristic notations in 93 percent of occurrences in the Crown of Aleppo — a rate of agreement that far exceeds that of other extant manuscripts of Ben Asher's time.[41] This strongly supports the claim in the Crown's dedication that the Crown was notated by Ben Asher.[42]

Finally, we know that Ben Asher was no longer alive in 989 because a manuscript from that year says of him, "May he rest in the Garden of Eden."[42]

Maimonides and the Crown

The second major issue in the debates over the Crown concerns the relationship between Maimonides and the Aleppo Codex, and, in particular, whether the Crown is the manuscript referred to by Maimonides in his writing. In *Sefer Ahava* (*Book of Adoration*), the second of the 14 books of the *Mishneh Torah*, Maimonides discusses the rules for writing a Torah scroll. In an unusual passage — unique not least for being written in the first person — Maimonides explains that he relied on a specific codex, both in his ruling on how a Torah scroll should be written and for writing his own Torah:

> *Because I saw serious errors in these matters in all the scrolls that I have seen, while authorities on the Masorah differ ... I deemed it fit to write here a list of the sections which are closed and which are open, and also the forms*

of the songs [of the Bible], so that all the scrolls may be corrected from, and compared with, them. The book which I relied upon to check the scrolls is the well-known codex in Egypt which contains the twenty-four books [of the Bible] and that had been in Jerusalem for several years, and upon which all relied, because it was proofread by Ben Asher, who worked on it carefully for many years and examined it again whenever it was being copied. This codex was the text upon which I relied in the Scroll of the Law that I myself wrote according to the rules.[43]

But is it possible to verify that the codex Maimonides used is indeed the one we now know as the Crown of Aleppo? The Aleppan Jews certainly identified the Crown as the one Maimonides consulted, but we cannot rely solely on this claim, since it obviously served to enhance the prestige of their prized possession. (This Aleppan claim is first attested to by Saadia ben David of Aden, a noted traveler who saw the Crown during a visit to Aleppo in the 15th century.)[44] Because Maimonides wrote in great detail about how to write a Torah scroll, had the Torah portions of the Crown survived, it would have been relatively easy to determine whether the codex on which he relied was in fact the Crown of Aleppo.[45]

In the century before the Crown was returned to Israel, this issue was hotly debated by scholars who based their claims solely on an examination of the few photographed pages of the codex. During this time several scholars, led by Heinrich Grätz,[46] tried to find evidence corroborating the contention of the Aleppan Jewish community. However, William Wickes,[47] among others, disputed that the Aleppo Codex could be attributed to Ben Asher, and thus that the text was the one to which Maimonides referred. After the Crown was returned to Israel in 1958, it became possible to reopen the debate. Even then, however, it was difficult to come to any definitive conclusions about this question, because only about five percent of the Torah portions of the Crown—the sections Maimonides would have consulted to determine the proper rules for copying the Torah text—had survived.

The controversy was further complicated by Umberto (Moshe David) Cassuto, the last non-Aleppan scholar to examine the Crown in its entirety. Cassuto (1883–1951) was a renowned Italian rabbi and Judaic scholar known for his expertise in biblical studies. He was educated at the University of Florence and the Rabbinical College. He taught at both institutions before joining the University of Rome. After anti-Jewish legislation was enacted in Italy in 1938, Cassuto was forced out of his faculty position at the University of Rome. He joined the faculty of Hebrew University in 1939,[48] and once in Jerusalem, he was asked to serve as editor of the university's new edition of the Bible.

At the time, there was great interest among Zionists and religious scholars alike in publishing a definitive edition of the Bible that would symbolically reclaim it for the Jewish people.[49] Up to this point, the most widely available printed editions of the Bible had been arranged either by Christians or Jewish apostates to Christianity. (The first printed Hebrew edition of the Bible in 1517, edited by the apostate Felix Pratensis, was dedicated to the Pope.)[50] Zionists saw the Bible not only as their title deed to Israel but also as a blueprint for the Jewish state's future. Jewish scholars meanwhile saw the opportunity to finally publish a corrective edition that conformed to Jewish traditions of chapter division, textual arrangement, and interpretation. At the symbolic level, the publication of such a volume in Israel would affirm that the Torah would once again "go forth from Zion" (Isa. 2:3).

The Crown was to figure prominently in this new scholarly edition of the Bible. Historian and Hashomer leader Yitzhak Ben-Zvi, later to serve as the second president of the State of Israel, had visited Aleppo in 1933, and was honored by the Jewish community leaders with a viewing of the Crown. Ben-Zvi and Hebrew University president Judah Magnes were eager to gain access to the Crown as a source for the new edition of the Bible. After a somewhat fitful beginning, during which the literature professor Yitzhak Shamosh initially attempted to acquire the codex, Professor Cassuto was chosen to travel to Aleppo in late 1943.

Cassuto would be the last scholar from outside the Aleppan community to see the intact Crown before it was damaged in 1947, and his conclusions regarding Maimonides' connection to the codex would confound scholars for years. In a December 27, 1947, letter to the German scholar Paul Kahle, Cassuto wrote that he did not believe Maimonides was referring to the Crown when he wrote his *Mishneh Torah,* but he did not elaborate on his conclusion.[51] He also wrote in a newspaper article that he did not believe that the manuscript was the one Maimonides referred to, "for technical reasons for which this is not the place."[52] He never publicly expanded on these reasons before he died in 1951, leaving many projects—including plans to publish his research on the Crown—uncompleted. For years, Cassuto's assessment was left undisputed, as no scholar could view the intact Crown to prove otherwise.

Once the Crown arrived in Israel in 1958, however, Moshe Goshen-Gottstein, a professor at Hebrew University, was able to disprove Cassuto's finding. Goshen-Gottstein argued that it was based on Maimonides' instructions about how the Song of Moses (*Haazinu*) in Deuteronomy 32 should be written in a Torah scroll. In most editions of the *Mishneh Torah,* Maimonides indicates that this poem should be written in 70 lines, with a space in the middle of every line such as that used for a closed section. He also specifies which word should begin each line. However, in the Crown's version of Deuteronomy 32, which fortunately survives, there are only 67 lines, and the first words of the lines are different from those specified by Maimonides. This would seem to be incontrovertible proof that Maimonides did not use the Crown as his model.

But Goshen-Gottstein reviewed several of the oldest manuscripts of the *Mishneh Torah,* including one that Maimonides himself signed.[53] He found that the most reliable text refers to 67 lines for *Haazinu* and also specifies the same beginning words as those found in the Crown. In addition, Yemenite scribes, who traditionally follow Maimonides' rulings particularly closely, also write the Song of Moses in 67 lines. Because no other known codex written before Maimonides' time arranges the Song of Moses in 67 lines, there can be little doubt that Maimonides was indeed referring to the Crown in his work.

Why then do printed versions of the *Mishneh Torah* mandate that the Song of Moses be written in 70 lines, not 67? Since it is technically difficult to write the lines this way, and since the tradition of 67 lines was not followed in most Jewish communities, it is likely that someone emended the text of the *Mishneh Torah* to reflect the more accepted practice, and this emended version became the more common one.[54]

Many years after Cassuto's death, his Aleppo journal was found in the Magnes Archives of the Central Archives for the History of the Jewish People in

The iron doors of the ark in the stone wall of the Cave of Elijah, where the Crown was safeguarded in the Great Synagogue of Aleppo. (*Courtesy of Beth Hatefutsoth, Photo Archive, Tel Aviv.*)

32

КАРАИМЫ.
Karaimes.

Abraham Firkovich (sitting) in an 1862 lithograph. From the left, his daughter, Milkah, his son-in-law, Gabriel, and an unknown Russian. (*Courtesy of the Library of the Jewish Theological Seminary.*)

Jerusalem. Cassuto's notes make it clear that he had indeed arrived at his controversial conclusion by comparing the Crown's Song of Moses against a printed edition of the *Mishneh Torah*. Thus Goshen-Gottstein's analysis was correct.[55] With Cassuto's concern addressed, we can state conclusively that the Crown is the codex that Maimonides referred to in the *Mishneh Torah*.

The Karaite Question

Even as the issue of the Crown's connection to Maimonides was laid to rest, another question remained to be resolved. Were Ben Asher and Ben Buya'a Karaites or Rabbanites?

The Karaites were a Jewish sect that emerged at the beginning of the 8th century C.E. Their doctrine is notable for its emphasis on the Bible as the sole and direct source of religious law, to the exclusion of the Oral Law (i.e., Rabbinic literature). The term "Karaite" (derived from "*Mikra*," the Hebrew word meaning "Scripture") was not applied to the sect until the 9th century; the group was initially known as the "Ananites," after its founder Anan ben David. The Karaites themselves, however, traced their origin to the first major split among the Jewish people at the time of King Jeroboam and, subsequently, to the Sadducees, whose leader, Tsadok, they felt preserved the true law—that is, the Written Law (the Bible) without the Oral Law.[56]

The Rabbanites, by contrast, were the spiritual successors to the Pharisees and the forerunners of today's mainstream branches of Judaism. The Rabbanites believed firmly that the Bible could not be fully interpreted without the Oral Law, as codified in the Mishnah and Talmud.

In time, the Karaites, despite their discounting of the Oral Law, developed their own extensive oral traditions, doctrines, and usages, which they called the Yoke of Tradition (*Sevel ha Yerusha*).[57] In part the Karaites' divergence from Rabbanite practice derived from their differences in biblical interpretation, which in some cases led them to adopt practices that were stricter than the Rabbanites' and in other cases ones that were more lenient.[58]

On one point at least, however, the Rabbanites and Karaites agreed: They both believed that the Bible was the word of God, and that it was absolutely essential that it be preserved and transmitted intact. For these reasons, both groups revered the Masoretes. Because of their emphasis on the biblical text, the Karaites held that public liturgical readings of the Torah could be made *only* from a punctuated, vocalized codex, not a traditional scroll. It was inconceivable to them that the Torah could have been given incomplete—that is, without the notations.[59] Indeed, the Crown's dedication records that the Karaite community of Jerusalem was authorized to use the codex for public readings on the three major holidays of Sukkot, Pesach, and Shavuot (the Festival of Tabernacles, Passover, and the Festival of Weeks).[60] By contrast, the Rabbanites insisted on the use of scrolls in liturgical contexts, on the grounds that this was how the Torah was originally given.

In the ninth century, Benjamin ben Moshe Nahawendi, the first scholar to use the term "Karaite," turned the idea of the free and independent study of the Bible into a basic principle of Karaism.[61] By the 10th century, Karaites were dedicating themselves with particular zeal to grammatical and Masoretic exegesis and study,[62] with Jerusalem serving as the center of their spiritual and scholarly activities.

The Karaites' conflict with the Rabbanites over the interpretation of biblical passages continued to spur the study of the Bible and the Hebrew language. Initially, the two groups were fierce competitors in what both sides saw as a zero-sum game to establish the primacy of their respective interpretations. However, by the time the Karaites acquired the Crown in the mid-11th century, the tensions had relaxed. (This latter period would come to an abrupt end with the capture of Jerusalem by Godfrey of Bouillon in 1099. The Crusaders, at least, did not distinguish between Rabbanites and Karaites; members of both communities were driven into a synagogue and burned alive.)[63]

The Crown's dedication describes how, in the middle of the 11th century, Israel ben Simha of Basra purchased the codex. He then donated it to the Karaite community in Jerusalem on condition that two brothers, Hezekiah and Josiah—prominent Karaites whom the dedication calls "princes"—take care of the Crown and make it available to any learned person, Karaite or Rabbanite, who wished to consult it.[64] Rabbi Meir Nehmad, who transcribed the dedication in the 1930s, established that Ben Simha also was a Karaite, but that the Crown had been in the hands of Rabbanites before he acquired it.[65] Does this mean the codex was originally written by Rabbanite scribes?

For decades, arguments have been made for and against the proposition that Ben Asher and Ben Buya'a were in fact Karaites. There is strong circumstantial evidence in favor of their Karaite identity. First, there is internal evidence drawn from the work of the Ben Asher Masoretes and from the Crown itself. For example, in his *Dikduke haTaamim,* Aharon ben Asher speaks about the halakhic authoritativeness of the entire Bible in terms that echo Karaite beliefs.[66] Furthermore, there is the evidence of Karaite tenets in the work of Aharon's father, Moshe ben Asher. In his introduction to the Cairo Codex, the elder Ben Asher states that the three parts of the Bible (the Torah, Prophets, and Writings) are equally authoritative for halakhic purposes—a classic Karaite position.[67] Similarly, the organization of the Crown of Aleppo, like that of the Cairo Codex and the Leningrad Codex, discussed later, does not follow the order set in the Talmud, which may reflect the Karaite's rejection of the Oral Law. [68] Finally, the Crown's dedication includes a prayer for the protection of the Temple. Some have argued that this must refer to the Karaites' temple in Jerusalem, as the Second Temple had been destroyed in 70 C.E.[69] By extension, this evidence would likely mean that Ben Buya'a, as Ben Asher's close collaborator, was a Karaite as well.

35

Second, external evidence also supports these claims. For example, Saadia Gaon wrote an anti-Karaite response, *Esa Meshali,* which criticized a Masorete named "Ben Asher." Given that Saadia Gaon and Aharon ben Asher were roughly contemporaries, this "Ben Asher" could well have been Aharon. In any case, we know of no other family of Masoretes named Ben Asher.[70]

References to the Ben Asher dynasty of Masoretes in contemporaneous texts are typically Karaite in wording, although not exclusively so—using, for example, terms such as "teacher" (*melamed*) and "enlightened one" (*maskil*).[71] In addition, the donor of the Cairo Codex, which was written by Aharon's father, Moshe ben Asher, used language that suggests he was a Karaite; it seems unlikely that such a patron would have given the work of a Rabbanite to the Karaite community of Cairo.[72]

Because the Crown was held by the Karaites of Jerusalem at the time the dedication was written, some scholars have concluded that the original owners, too, must have been Karaites; had Rabbanites possessed the Crown from the outset, they would not have permitted its transfer into Karaite hands. But by the 11th century, relations between the Rabbanites and the Karaites had greatly improved. Indeed, the stipulation allowing both Karaites and Rabbanites full access to the codex is a testament to the cordial relations between the two groups at that point.

In fact, such a transfer is quite plausible. If the Crown had been originally held by Rabbanites, the spiritual leader of the Yeshiva of the Land of Israel—the *gaon* or exilarch—would have personally controlled the codex. Perhaps not coincidentally, the *gaon* during this period (1025–1051), Shlomo ben Yehuda, frequently enlisted the help of the Karaites in his political battles. In addition, Ben Yehuda and the two Karaite princes Hezekiah and Josiah, to whose specific care the Crown was commended, each traced their lineage back to King David through Jehoiachin. We know from letters found in the Cairo Genizah that these men considered each other, whatever their personal differences, members of the same elite.

Some scholars have argued that Maimonides, a known opponent of the Karaites, would not have relied on the Crown if he believed it was tainted by Karaite authorship. Yet Maimonides praises the Crown strictly for its textual accuracy, not as a religious document. Furthermore, he is strangely circumspect about the origins of the codex. He refers to it as "the well-known codex in Egypt which contains the twenty-four books [of the Bible] and that had been in Jerusalem for several years, and upon which all relied, because it was proofread by Ben Asher."[73] And, while he specifically endorsed the arrangement of open and closed sections and the writing of the songs, he did not reference the Crown's orthography, vowels, accents, or Masoretic notes. He did not say whose work he considered authoritative on those points or whose work he would not have accepted.

Evidence that Ben Buya'a and Ben Asher were Rabbanites has also been proposed by various scholars. They point out that the colophon to Shlomo Ben Buya'a's codex found in Čūfut-Kale contains none of the textual code phrases

Karaites typically used to indicate their affiliation. Had Ben Buya'a been a Karaite, he would certainly have asserted that identity, and such phrases would be found in the colophon.[74] Furthermore, if Ben Buya'a was a Rabbanite, Ben Asher was probably also a Rabbanite. Given the strained relations between the two groups at the time the Crown was written, it would be unlikely to find a Rabbanite scribe collaborating with a Karaite annotator on the manuscript. Overall, the evidence on both sides of the debate remains circumstantial, and this fascinating question must remain open.

The Story of Abraham Firkovich

The question of the Crown's possible Karaite provenance is not simply an intellectual exercise, despite the lack of conclusive evidence from the time of the codex's writing. Instead, the Karaite question was to play a significant role in shaping historians' perceptions of the codex's authenticity for hundreds of years.

37

We will return to a more detailed description of the codex's journey later, but first we must digress from the chronology to follow the trail of a 19th-century Karaite named Abraham Firkovich, who was to play a vital role in the Crown's history.

In the years after the Crusades, as Jews were scattered ever farther from Israel, Rabbanite Jews predominated in most parts of the world. By the 17th and 18th centuries, two of the remaining centers of Karaite activity were in Crimea and Lithuania, where Karaites continued to live side-by-side with Rabbanites.[75]

The landscape began to change, however, when Russia seized control of Crimea in 1783 and Lithuania in 1793. Although many other minorities who lived in these regions fled in fear, the Crimean Jews—Karaite and Rabbanite—remained. To that point, both groups had generally considered each other Jews. Even the most violent polemics were treated by both sides as internal Jewish quarrels. Certainly, non-Jews did not distinguish between the groups in terms of either privileges and rights or taxes and discrimination.[76]

In 1795, however, Empress Catherine II imposed a double tax on Jews, and it was at that point that the destinies of the Rabbanites and Karaites began

A Firkovich family photograph. From the left: Abraham Firkovich, his wife, Hanna, his son in-law, Gabriel, and his daughter, Milkah. (*Courtesy of Michail Kizilov, from the library of the Lithuanian Academy of Sciences.*)

to diverge in earnest. The Karaites sent a delegation to the empress to argue that they should be exempt from the tax on the grounds that they were not in fact Jews but rather Karaites "of the Old Testament faith." On June 8, 1795, Catherine agreed to exclude the Karaites from the discriminatory tax and also permitted them to acquire land.[77]

In 1827, the Crimean Karaites asserted their separateness again, this time gaining exemption, together with the Crimean Tatars, from the forced conscription law, to which the Crimean Rabbanites remained subject. In the following year, this dispensation was extended to the Karaites of Lithuania and Volhynia. In 1837, the Karaites achieved a change in their official designation from Jews to simply Karaites. In 1840, they were put on equal footing with Muslims and were granted an independent church statute. Finally, in 1863, the Karaites were granted rights equal to those of the native Russian population.[78]

The Karaite intellectual who most influenced these later rulings was a man named Abraham Firkovich. Firkovich (1786–1874), was born in a small village outside Luck, Poland, studied the principles of the Karaite religion, and then settled in Crimea, perhaps in search of greater opportunities. In 1830, the head of the Historical Society of Odessa, Simha Babovich, recommended Firkovich to Prince Mikhail Semenovich Vorontsov, the governor general of Crimea, as a scholar who could best provide the government with information regarding Karaite history and their claims to a separate identity from the Jews.[79]

Vorontsov issued a writ authorizing Firkovich to acquire whatever materials he needed for his research. This gathering of evidence was to become a lifelong obsession for Firkovich, who in the end collected more than 15,000 Hebrew manuscripts, which he subsequently sold to the Imperial Library (now known as the Russian National Library) in St. Petersburg.[80]

In seeking to ingratiate themselves with the Russian rulers, the Karaites sought to demonstrate that they, unlike the reviled Jews, were not implicated in the death of Jesus. To this end, Firkovich forged the dates on gravestones in Crimean cemeteries to make it appear as though the Karaites had arrived in Crimea before the beginning of the Common Era.[81]

Firkovich's next task was to demonstrate that the Karaites were in fact responsible for the positive contributions to society heretofore attributed to the Jews, particularly in the areas of Hebrew and biblical studies. By purchase, theft, and intimidation, Firkovich acquired Jewish manuscripts and forged their colophons to suggest that the works were authored by Karaites. In 1859, he sent the Imperial Library in St. Petersburg a detailed description of the manuscripts he had acquired, noting their importance and asking for 25,000 rubles in exchange for the collection. In 1863, after some negotiations, the director of the library agreed to this price and acquired the collection.[82]

Even after receiving word that the Karaites had achieved full civil and political rights in 1863, Firkovich continued his quest. He set out for the Middle East to acquire more manuscripts. On October 3, 1863, he landed in Jaffa, and from there he made his way to Jerusalem. Within a month, he was headed north, and on November 11, he entered the gates of Aleppo. Not long after arriving in the city, he set to work trying to acquire the Crown.[83]

In a letter to Simha Babovich's son Nahamu, Firkovich described what happened next. He approached the Turkish governor and showed him letters of authorization he had received from the Russian and Ottoman Empires. The pasha issued him a *firman*, a decree of protection and empowerment, and authorized an armored guard of soldiers to assist him. Firkovich was allowed access to certain mosques that had formerly been synagogues so that he could examine them for Jewish inscriptions and artifacts. In particular, there had been rumors that Jews had hidden a manuscript in the Jamiya al-Hayat, near the ancient citadel of Aleppo, when it was still a synagogue.[84] When these leads brought no results, Firkovich paid the sexton of the Great Synagogue to allow him to see the Crown. He quickly recognized that the Crown's dedication was identical to that of a manuscript in the synagogue of Rabbi Moshe Isserlis (the RaMA) in Cracow. Before Firkovich was able to view the codex a second time, the elders of the community were alerted, and they barred him from seeing it again.

The furtive—even illicit—manner by which Firkovich sought out the Crown appears to have affected the way the codex was handled thereafter. According to the Aleppan rabbi Yitzhak Shchebar, the Crown and three other ancient codices of the community were soon placed in an iron box (in a section of the synagogue known as the Cave of Elijah), in part because outsiders reportedly had tried to acquire the Crown.[85] Although Shchebar did not mention Firkovich by name, it seems likely that Firkovich's attempt to acquire the Crown made the Aleppo community even more leery than it had been about allowing access to anyone from outside the community.

Firkovich's exploits also influenced perceptions of the Crown in a more damaging way. His record of forging documents and colophons to claim Karaite provenance for hundreds of manuscripts meant every artifact he touched was suspect, including the Crown of Aleppo. Although he saw it only briefly, Firkovich later claimed to the Jerusalem rabbi Yaakov Sapir that the Crown's colophon attributed the codex to Shlomo ben Yeroham (born about 910), not Shlomo ben Buya'a. Ben Yeroham, an important 10th-century Karaite scholar and the author of *Milhamot Adonai,* was famous for his vicious attacks against Saadia Gaon, the great Rabbanite leader. Born in Fostat, Ben Yeroham had moved to Aleppo and lived there until his death. Firkovich was probably also responsible for adding a copy of the codex dedication to a manuscript in the Karaite synagogue in Jerusalem, again attributing the codex to Ben Yeroham.[86]

Firkovich's motives were obvious. If he could show that Aharon ben Asher, acknowledged by all as the greatest master of the Masorah, was, like Ben Yeroham, a Karaite, he would demonstrate Karaite superiority over the Rabbanites in the areas of Hebrew and biblical scholarship.

At least in part due to Firkovich's forgeries, the prominent historian Abraham Harkavy became one of the first scholars to attack the provenance and antiquity of the Crown. Harkavy, born in Novogrudok, Byelorussia, in 1835, had been educated at *yeshivot* in Lithuania and prominent universities in St. Petersburg, Berlin, and Paris. Although a highly qualified scholar, he could not secure an academic post in Russia as a Jew. In 1870 he began work at the Department of Jewish Literature and Oriental Manuscripts at the Imperial Library in St. Petersburg, where he had the opportunity to examine closely the manuscripts Firkovich had collected. He concluded that at least parts of the manuscripts were forgeries. In 1875, shortly after Firkovich's death, Harkavy and the German scholar Hermann Strack published their case against Firkovich in the *Catalog*

41

der hebraischen Bibelhandschriften. Strack's *A. Firkowitsch und seine Entdeckungen* and Harkavy's *Altjudische Denkmaler aus der Krim,* both published in 1876, further disputed Firkovich's claims.[87]

Ultimately, Harkavy and Strack's works influenced a great number of historians, who similarly grew to doubt the authenticity of the Crown.

The Significance of the Crown

Despite Abraham Firkovich's unscholarly and even at times nefarious methods of acquiring and forging parts of ancient manuscripts, scholars owe him a debt of gratitude for having uncovered the most highly regarded biblical codex extant, apart from the Crown of Aleppo. Known as the Leningrad Codex, this manuscript has, unlike the Crown, survived intact, making it the oldest complete codex of the Bible.

According to its colophon, the Leningrad Codex was completed in Cairo in 1008 by Shmuel ben Yaakov. Firkovich acquired the book from an unknown location and brought it to Odessa in 1838. He later sold it to the Imperial Library, where it was accessioned as Firkovich B 19 A.

With access to the Crown restricted for hundreds of years, modern biblical scholars resorted to using the Leningrad Codex for several authoritative editions of the Bible. Paul E. Kahle and Rudolf Kittel used the Leningrad Codex for the third edition of the *Biblia Hebraica* (1937).[88] It was used as well for the fourth edition, known as the *Biblia Hebraica Stuttgartensia,* which was published in 1977, nearly two decades after the Crown was recovered, and it remains the core text for the fifth edition, the *Biblia Hebraica Quinta* (forthcoming). The Jewish Publication Society's Hebrew-English Tanakh and Aron Dotan's *Bible for the Israel Defense Forces* are also based on the Leningrad Codex text.

By carefully examining the Leningrad Codex, scholars have gained a precise understanding of the features that, by comparison, make the Crown of Aleppo the more significant of the two works. The Leningrad Codex closely resembles the Crown on matters of vocalization and accentuation. But it is not precise in its use of full and defective spellings, and in many cases the text does not conform to the Masoretic notes in the manuscript itself.[89] Some believe the

Professor Umberto Cassuto in his study, Jerusalem 1940. (*Courtesy of the Ben-Zvi Institute, Jerusalem.*)

Aleppan scholars inside the Great Synagogue at the beginning of the 20th Century. (*Courtesy of the Ben-Zvi Institute, Jerusalem.*)

Leningrad Codex scribe was attempting — unsuccessfully — to conform a manuscript from a different Tiberian tradition to the more exacting requirements of Aharon Ben Asher's meticulous work. The fact that the Leningrad Codex scribe felt the need to "harmonize" the original text with the Crown suggests that, just a few short decades after Ben Asher's death, his codex was considered the gold standard.[90]

The Crown's dedication dates the original text to the early decades of the 10th century, making it the earliest known codex of the entire Bible. (By way of comparison, the Dead Sea Scrolls were written by the 1st century B.C.E., and the earliest extant Torah scroll dates from the 12th century.) Scholars have substantiated the 10th-century dating by analyzing many technical details of the work.[91]

It is clear that the Crown, though now incomplete, is the oldest such codex in existence.[92] But was it also the first complete codex of the Bible? Given the great numbers of Jewish communities laid waste over the centuries, it is impossible to prove this; with each community destroyed, no doubt many possible links to the texts of antiquity have been lost as well. But no earlier or contemporaneous source mentions any such complete Masoretic codex penned by a master Masorete or anyone else. In fact, all our sources point to Ben Asher's work as the crowning achievement in the development of biblical manuscripts.[93]

The Crown's preeminence is also clear from additional sources. For one thing, other Masoretes, most notably the author of the Leningrad Codex, made a point of stating that their works followed Ben Asher's definitive text and notational system. For another, as early as the 10th century, we see Ben Asher's text referred to as *al-Taj*, or "the Crown" — that is, the codex of codices.[94] Thus, barring the highly unlikely discovery of an earlier complete codex, we can assume that the Crown of Aleppo is the authoritative distillation of the Masorah, the first and preeminent exemplar of its caliber.

The fact that the Crown is the work of Ben Asher and Ben Buya'a further establishes the codex's reputation. The more important contributor was the master Masorete Aharon ben Asher, who reviewed Ben Buya'a's scribal work to ensure that it conformed to the Masoretic tradition. Thus, for example, he made clear determinations regarding the text's division into sections and the line divisions of the songs (in Exodus 15 and Deuteronomy 32). We must attribute these distinctive features to Ben Asher, because we know they appear differently in the Čūfut-Kale codex written by Ben Buya'a and annotated by his relative.[95]

Also, Maimonides' reliance on the Crown solidified its singular status. He did not otherwise endorse the Crown, except implicitly, by saying that he relied on the Crown in writing his own Torah scroll.[96] Nonetheless, in a matter of particular halakhic concern to him — the open and closed sections — Maimonides explicitly affirmed the superiority of the Crown's text.[97]

To scholars, of course, it is the Crown's meticulous accuracy and precise internal consistency that make it the premier Masoretic text.[98] A good correlation between the text and the notes is a key test of the quality of a Masoretic codex, but most codices invariably contain spelling and other discrepancies. Several codices omit the notes altogether or even turn them into ornamentation. Some Masoretes faithfully copied the proper annotations but neglected to check them against the passages to which they corresponded to ensure that the accentuation and vocalization in the text were accurate. The Crown is the only example in existence of a codex with almost complete harmony between text and notes.[99]

As one scholar points out:

> In the manuscript known as the Leningrad Codex, there are more than 250 places in the Prophets where the scribe erred with respect to full and defective spellings. In the Cairo manuscript of the Prophets [by Moshe ben Asher] there are about 130 errors in full and defective spellings. However, in the Aleppo Codex there are two places in the Prophets where it is clear that the scribe erred with respect to full and defective spellings, and five where it appears that he erred.[100]

45

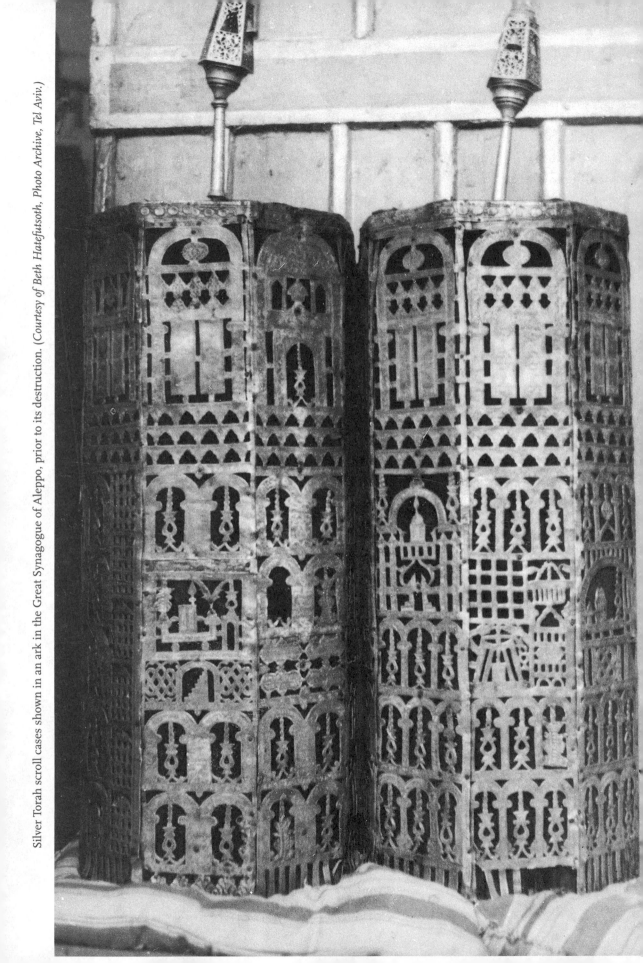

Silver Torah scroll cases shown in an ark in the Great Synagogue of Aleppo, prior to its destruction. (*Courtesy of Beth Hatefutsoth, Photo Archive, Tel Aviv.*)

3

THE CROWN'S HISTORY FROM 11TH-CENTURY JERUSALEM TO 20TH-CENTURY ALEPPO

The Crown in Jerusalem

Prior to the Muslim conquest of 638, Jews had been barred from entering Jerusalem by its Christian rulers, and Tiberias had served instead as the center of Jewish learning and pilgrimage. Once they were allowed to resettle in Jerusalem, however, Jews—among them a fair number of Karaites—began to return. The first period of Muslim rule was to stretch over the better part of five centuries (638–1099), and Jerusalem at the beginning of the 11th century was a politically stable, tridenominational, multiethnic city.

Contemporaneous accounts offer little evidence of the Jewish community in Jerusalem during this time, but in the late 19th century a treasure trove of documents, including personal letters, were discovered in the Cairo Genizah (the depository for worn books and religious documents of the Ben Ezra Synagogue in Fostat, Egypt) that attested to the vitality of the city's large Jewish community. From these accounts we learn that Jerusalem remained the center of Jewish religious worship while Ramle served as the administrative capital for the southern part of Israel.

Financially, however, Jewish Jerusalem was not strong. The community mainly relied on income from tourism and charitable donations. Jewish travelers made their way to Jerusalem particularly during the three major pilgrimage holidays (the *Shalosh Regalim* of Pesach, Shavuot, and Sukkot). The visitors stayed at Jewish inns, ate at kosher establishments, and frequently brought donations from their home communities. Outside of the holiday periods, however, Jewish Jerusalem's finances suffered. One letter found in the Cairo Genizah reports: "Many have come here [to Jerusalem] rich and have been reduced to poverty." In another poignant letter, a man tells his son-in-law to return to Jerusalem, because it is better "to eat onions in Jerusalem than chicken in Egypt."[1]

Although impoverished, Jerusalem prided itself on its status as the spiritual center of Jewish life, and the Yeshiva of the Land of Israel relocated to Jerusalem from Tiberias. The exact date of this move is unknown,[2] but it is possible that the Crown was transferred to Jerusalem during the move of the yeshiva or soon afterward.

The Crown's safekeeping in Jerusalem, however, grew precarious as the city's fate became more uncertain. In 1071, the Sunni Turkish Seljuks attacked Jerusalem and took possession from the Shiite Fatimids. This began a period of unrest that saw the collapse of law and order in the city and a brutally suppressed insurrection in 1077. In 1098 the Fatimids recaptured Jerusalem, but their control was short lived. By this point, the Crusaders were on the march.

In 1095, Pope Urban II had called on Christians around the world to "retake the Holy Land." By 1099, they had reached their ultimate destination and, after a 39-day siege, they captured Jerusalem. The Crusaders marked their entry into the city with a ferocious massacre that lasted four days. Almost all of the city's Jews were killed.[3] When Benjamin of Tudela visited Jerusalem in 1170, he reported that only four Jews remained in the city.[4]

Where was the Crown during this period? The record is not clear. The codex's dedication had been written around 1050,[5] decades before either the Seljuks or the Crusaders had reached Jerusalem. It is not known whether the Crown was stolen by the Seljuks or the Crusaders.[6] The Crusaders, however, from their earlier experience in ransacking the Jewish communities of Europe, would have known the value of Hebrew books and the price that would be paid for their ransom. In any event, we know from a postscript to the codex's dedication that the Crown was next ransomed to Fostat, the heart of medieval Egypt.[7]

The Crown in Fostat

When 'Amr ibn al-'Āṣ conquered Egypt in the name of Islam in 641 c.e., he built Fostat — situated on the east bank of the Nile, near the site of an ancient Greco-Coptic town — as his new capital. By the 9th century, Fostat had surpassed Alexandria in size. In June 969 c.e., the Fatamids took over Fostat and built their imperial city nearby. Because it was built under the ascendancy of the planet Mars, or *al-Qahir* in Arabic, the Fatamids called their new city *Al-Qahirah* (which became known as Cairo in English).[8] After Ṣalāḥ al-Dīn (Saladin) rose to power in Egypt around 1172, he connected the two cities, which eventually merged into one.

49

Fostat in the 12th century hummed with commerce and activity. The city's Jewish community — which according to local tradition had originated at the time of the settlement of Jeremiah in Egypt[9] — was located close to the center of town and eventually concentrated in the Zuwayla district north of al-Jadida Street. Here, in the Jewish quarter, stood the Ben Ezra Synagogue; its genizah was situated in one corner of the building.[10]

Fortunately for scholarship, the Cairenes threw all sorts of Hebrew writings in their genizah, not just sacred documents, and so when the storeroom was rediscovered by scholars in the 19th century, almost 300,000 documents and fragments of documents were found there.[11] One fascinating letter from April 1100 describes how the Jews of Ashkelon, with money from the Jews of Egypt, were able to ransom captives and a large number of Hebrew books from the Crusaders:

> *News still reaches us continuously of those who were redeemed from the Franks and remained in Ashkelon. Some are in danger of dying from want of food and clothing and from exhaustion. Others remained in captivity, of whom*

some were killed with all manner of torture out of sheer lust to murder before the eyes of others who were spared. We did not hear of a single man of Israel in such danger without exerting ourselves to do all that was in our power to save him ... All this is in addition to the money that was borrowed and spent in order to buy back two hundred and thirty Bible codices, a hundred other volumes, and eight Torah Scrolls. All these are communal property and are now in Ashkelon.[12]

Although we cannot be sure the Crown was among these books, another discovery in the genizah revealed some important clues. In a list of books held in the synagogue's library in 1186–1187, reference is made to a Bible codex called *"al-Taj"* ("the Crown") — precisely the Arabic name for the codex we know as the Crown of Aleppo. The genizah also contained a letter from the synagogue council to an unknown donor who was contributing to the restoration of a complete Bible codex referred to as *"Akhu mashaf al-Taj"* or "the brother of the codex [referred to as] *al-Taj.*" Clearly, the Taj was considered a very important document. Interestingly, the date of the list coincides with the period of Maimonides' residence in Fostat.

Maimonides' Descendants and the Crown's Transfer to Aleppo

Moses Maimonides was born in Cordoba, in Andalucia, around 1138. Nine years later, he and his family fled the area as the Almohads (*al-Muwahhidun*), a fundamentalist Muslim sect, took control and began forced conversions to Islam.[13] After living for a decade in various parts of southern Spain, the family, by 1159 or 1160, had crossed the Strait of Gibraltar and established residence in Fez, in what is today Morocco. In 1165, Maimonides lived briefly in Israel, and by 1166, he had arrived in Fostat, where he would remain until his death in 1204.

Maimonides was a trained physician, and in time he was appointed chief physician to the vizier in Cairo; he also treated patients in Fostat. By night, he studied Torah and Talmud. In 1168, Maimonides completed his commentary on the Mishnah, which he followed with his *Mishneh Torah*. At some point in this period, he had the opportunity to study the codex of Ben Asher.

After Maimonides' death in 1204, his only son, Abraham ben Moshe (1186–1237), became the leader of the Egyptian Jewish community. After Abraham's death, his son David became the leader of the community, as in time did David's son, Abraham. When the Mamluks took control of Fostat in 1252, the position of the Jews declined considerably. In 1375, David, the great-great-great grandson of Maimonides, moved to Syria. He stayed briefly in Damascus but ultimately settled in Aleppo, where he apparently remained until his death around 1410.[14]

Although there is no evidence that Maimonides or his family ever had possession of the Crown, some scholars have speculated that the codex was among the documents Rabbi David took with him to Aleppo.[15] Indeed, at his death, Maimonides had specified that certain of his manuscripts were to remain in the possession of his family, to be passed down to the eldest son in each generation.

But if the Crown was in Aleppo in 1375 and was so prized and revered, why was no mention made of it during this period? Further, Aleppo's Great Synagogue was destroyed and rebuilt in the 1400s, but again, no mention of the Crown's presence in Aleppo at that point has been found in connection with the rebuilding.[16] (In fact, a song in praise of the synagogue inscribed on a silver Torah case as late as 1710 makes no mention of the Crown.)[17] Considering what we know of the esteem in which the Crown was held, these omissions seem very odd.

Yet we know that the Crown was in Aleppo by 1479. In that year, Saadia ben David of Aden visited Aleppo. This distinguished scholar, who wrote commentaries on the Torah, the Prophets, and the *Mishneh Torah*, examined the Crown at length and wrote:

> The codex which the Giant of Blessed Memory [Maimonides] used as his authority is still today in the town of Tsova [i.e., Aram Tsova or Aleppo] and is called al-Taj [the Crown]. It is written on parchment with three columns of writing to every page. At the end is written: "I, Aharon ben Asher collated it ... "[18]

After this point, the codex is occasionally mentioned in the records of travelers to Aleppo. For example, it is described by the Safed scholar Rabbi Yosef Ashkenazi, who saw it during his visit in the latter half of the 16th century.[19] The English traveler Alexander Russell, who visited Aleppo in the 18th century, noted the prayer for the Temple in the dedication,[20] which the community

51

cited as proof of the Crown's dating to the period before the destruction of the Temple in Jerusalem.

And yet, we still do not have a clear sense of why or how the Aleppan Jewish community came to possess the codex. Some have theorized that the Crown ended up in Aleppo because of Maimonides' close connection to the city in his lifetime and after his death in 1204. They cite at least four instances of circumstantial evidence for their claim. First, Maimonides spoke highly of Aleppo in a letter to the Jews of Lunel, France, in which he described the city as the only place in Israel and Syria where Jewish scholarship thrived.[21] Second, his star pupil, Yosef ben Yehuda ibn Shimon, to whom he dedicated the *Guide for the Perplexed,* moved to Aleppo and established his school there. (Yosef ben Yehuda was also appointed the court physician of El-Dahir Gazi, the ruler of Aleppo and son of Saladin.) Third, Maimonides' study method, as outlined in the introduction to the *Mishneh Torah,* and as described in a letter to Ben Aknin, was quickly adopted by the Jewish community in Aleppo. Finally, as previously noted, Maimonides' descendants ultimately moved to Aleppo,[22] quite possibly bringing the Crown with them.

It has also been argued that the Crown was stolen or otherwise taken without permission from its rightful owners in Fostat.[23] This version of events would explain several curious facts about the Crown. First, as we have noted, there is no record of the codex's arrival in Aleppo—no account of who brought it, or of when, why, or how they did so. Second, the Crown's existence in Aleppo is unremarked upon even after its arrival. Only through the report of an outsider, Saadia ben David of Aden, do we learn that the codex was in Aleppo no later than 1479. Third, the Aleppan community appears to have been particularly concerned about the safety of the Crown. They were deeply suspicious that outsiders would try to take the Crown and very hesitant to allow the Crown to be viewed by outsiders or even by members of their own community, despite the clear edict in the dedication that the Crown should be made available for all scholars to review. The language of admonition (the so-called curses, described later) was added after the Crown had been completed, possibly in Aleppo. The Aleppans' secrecy may have originated from their fears that the codex would be reclaimed by its rightful owner or from their remorse over having stolen the Crown or accepted stolen goods.

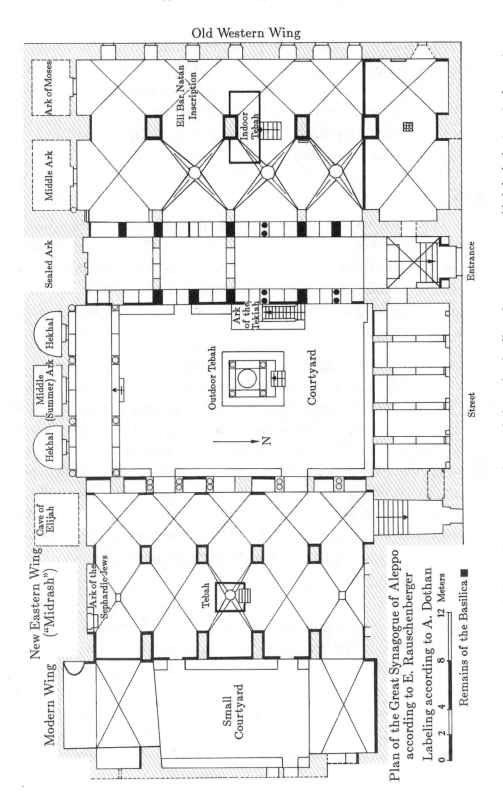

Old Western Wing

Ark of Moses

Middle Ark

Sealed Ark

Eli Bar Natan Inscription

Indoor Tebah

Entrance

Hekhal
Hekhal

Middle (Summer) Ark

Ark of the Tebah

Outdoor Tebah

Courtyard

N

Street

Cave of Elijah

New Eastern Wing ("Midrash")

Ark of the Sephardic Jews

Tebah

Modern Wing

Small Courtyard

Plan of the Great Synagogue of Aleppo
according to E. Rauschenberger
Labeling according to A. Dothan

0 2 4 8 12 Meters

■ Remains of the Basilica

Floor plan of the Great Synagogue of Aleppo. This drawing, made in 1956, shows details of how the synagogue most likely looked prior to its destruction in 1947. (*Courtesy of Beth Hatefutsoth, Photo Archive, Tel Aviv.*)

It is at this point that we must gain perspective on the cultural and historical forces that shaped the Jewish community of Aleppo, so that we can better understand the next episodes in the Crown's history. However they obtained it, Aleppan Jews would control the Crown for nearly five hundred years, and Syria's history and the history of Aleppo in particular played important roles in shaping the Crown's destiny.

Syria

Syria is known in Arabic as *Bilad al-Sham*, or "the region on one's left hand." If one faces east on Arabian Peninsula, Syria lies on the left, and Yemen (*Yaman*, or "the region on one's right hand") is on the right. In the early Islamic era, the territory of *Bilad al-Sham* encompassed what today would be referred to as Greater Syria—that is, the modern states of Syria, Israel, Lebanon, and Jordan, as well as what is now Hatay, Turkey.[24]

Modern Syria falls naturally into two geographical regions: the western Levantine area bordering the Mediterranean and the eastern inland area. The western region is characterized by a diverse geography and a maritime climate.[25] Inland from the narrow coastal plain are mountain ranges running roughly north to south. The southern region encompasses the Lebanon and Anti-Lebanon Mountains, including Mount Hermon, and between these two ranges, on the border between Lebanon and Syria, lies the Bekaa Valley.[26] From the eastern slopes of these hills and mountains begin the steppes and deserts demarcating the eastern region of Syria, where several major cities of modern Syria, including Damascus and Aleppo, are located.[27]

Aleppo

The city of Aleppo has a long and rich history, beginning with the legends of its founding. According to local lore, the city received its name when Abraham stopped in Aleppo on his way to Israel from Haran almost 4,000 years ago. Abraham pastured his sheep on the hills, and then, as an act of charity, he distributed the milk (in Arabic, *"halab"*) to the city's poor. Since that time, the city has been called "Haleb" in Arabic and Aramaic (from which we derive the corrupted pronunciation "Aleppo" in English).[28] The noted medieval traveler

Petahia of Regensburg, among others, also recounts this legend.[29] But another, if less romantic, possibility is that the name derived from the white (in Aramaic, *"halaba"*) soil and marble found in the area.

Because the modern city of Aleppo occupies the same site as the ancient city, it has remained largely untouched by archaeologists. But historical records recount that the city was conquered by the Romans in 64 B.C.E.; it subsequently became part of the Byzantine Empire until the Arab conquest of the city in 637. For the next six centuries, numerous Muslim conquerors fought over control of the city.

In 1260, the citadel, walls, and Grand Mosque of Aleppo were destroyed during the first Mongol invasion.[30] In 1280, the Mongols pillaged and burned the sultan's palace as well as mosques, madrasas (schools), and the homes of the emirs (nobility). Mongols also besieged the city in 1300 and in 1301; in 1400, after a period of relative quiet, Aleppo was invaded and decimated yet again by the Mongols.[31]

The Ottomans conquered Aleppo in 1517. According to Ottoman censuses, Aleppo had a population of about 67,000 in 1520 and 57,000 a decade later.[32] Aleppo's industries revolved around tanning, cotton carding, spinning, bleaching, dyeing, and weaving. The city was particularly renowned for its soap, although copper, iron, ceramics, paper, glass, saddles, and weaponry were also produced there.[33]

Under Ottoman rule, Aleppo was the administrative capital of its own province, reporting directly to the Sublime Porte in Constantinople, and thus of equal status with Damascus.[34] It also served as Ottoman Syria's leading commercial center from 1517 to about 1800.[35] During this time, the city was a trading hub between Iran and Iraq to the east and Europe to the west. Caravans passed through Aleppo, and many ships docked at the nearby Mediterranean port of Alexandretta.[36]

Historically, Aleppo's economy was tied primarily to the regions to its north and east; it served as the center of commerce for northern Syria, northwest Iraq, and in particular southeast Anatolia, Aleppo's largest supplier of raw materials and foodstuffs.[37] By the late 18th century, however, Aleppo had lost much of its trading role, as European merchants traveling to China, India, and elsewhere in Asia began to sail the Cape of Good Hope instead of trekking overland.[38] The fortunes of the city declined yet further when the Suez Canal was opened in 1869, shifting the important trade routes from Syria to Egypt. While English and Italian merchants continued to visit Aleppo, they came to sell manufactured European goods, not to purchase local goods.

After the end of World War I and the collapse of the Ottoman Empire, the Sykes-Picot Agreement between Britain and France, and, later, the French Mandate of 1923–1943 fixed the boundary between Syria and Turkey just north of Aleppo, thereby cutting the city off from its traditional agricultural and economic hinterland.[39] Damascus soon surpassed Aleppo economically and politically. After 1928, modern industries sprang up in Aleppo, but they were for the most part focused on mechanizing the region's traditional handicrafts of tanning, weaving, and soap making.[40] As colonial and Mandate-era Syria continued mainly to export its raw materials, France exploited Aleppo primarily as a market for its manufactured goods.[41] With the Sanjak of Alexandretta's absorption as a Turkish province in 1939, Aleppo could no longer access the Mediterranean port of Alexandretta (now known as Iskenderun), and its economic troubles deepened.

Despite its economic decline, however, Aleppo's population during the French mandatory period was slightly larger than that of Damascus. In 1932, it had 232,000 people compared to Damascus's 216,000; at the close of the Mandate, its population was 319,867, while Damascus's population numbered 286,310.[42]

The Jewish Community of Aleppo

Although it is not known when Jews first came to Aleppo, an ancient tradition dates the community to the period after the destruction of the First Temple in 586 B.C.E., which would make it among the most ancient of continuous Jewish settlements in the Diaspora.

In fact, the Jewish presence in Syria is well documented from the Roman period on. The historian Josephus, for example, recorded how Ezra the Scribe was commanded by Xerxes in the 5th century B.C.E. to appoint judges among

The ancient main entrance doors of the Great Synagogue of Aleppo. The large iron doors were unadorned so as to not attract attention from passersby. (*Courtesy of Beth Hatefutsoth, Photo Archive, Tel Aviv.*)

the Jews to hold court in all of Syria and Phoenicia. Josephus stated that "for as the Jewish nation is widely dispersed over all the habitable earth among its inhabitants, so it is very much intermingled with Syria."[43]

For centuries Jews played a prominent role in the life of Aleppo. But it was in the area of Jewish scholarship that Aleppan Jews were most prominent. For hundreds of years, rabbis visited Aleppo to study and teach. The great Jewish philosopher and philologist Saadia Gaon came to the city in 921 and remained for an extended period.[44] The community's numbers were bolstered in the 10th century by Jews fleeing political chaos in Iraq.[45]

In the 11th century, rabbis Barukh ben Yitzhak and Barukh ben Shmuel were recognized as leaders of Aleppo's Jews. Ben Yitzhak's commentary on the Talmud was widely read, and parts of it are still extant. Maimonides praised Aleppo as a center of Torah study that exceeded that of Israel and all the rest of Syria,[46] and Maimonides' own descendants ultimately left Egypt for Aleppo. Similarly, Yehuda ben Shlomo Alharizi, the noted rabbi, traveler, poet, and translator of the *Guide for the Perplexed*, praised Aleppo at length after his visit there in 1217.[47]

Spanish Jews fleeing Muslim persecution from the 10th to the 12th centuries also played a significant role in energizing Aleppo's Jewish community. These refugees brought new knowledge of medicine, the arts, and printing, and with their capacious understanding of Jewish law, they initiated a revival of Torah study. The already prominent Aleppan yeshivas were particular beneficiaries of this influx.

The fortunes of Aleppo's Jewish community rose and fell with those of the city. During the upheavals of the 13th and 14th centuries, Aleppo's Jews suffered along with the rest of the population, and the Great Synagogue was largely destroyed in the Mongol invasion of 1400. Under Ottoman rule, however, life in Aleppo became more settled, and the Jewish community began to revive.

After the beginning of the Spanish Inquisition in 1492, a second wave of Spanish Jews reached Aleppo. The Sephardi newcomers were welcomed, but their immigration led to some early friction with the established Jewish community. Initially, the Spanish Jews kept themselves apart, retaining their customs and the Ladino language instead of embracing the local customs and the Judeo-Arabic spoken by the indigenous Syrian Jews known as *Musta'arabim,* or Arabized Jews. Jewish traders from Italy arrived in the city in the late 17th and early 18th centuries, and French Jewish educators, traders, and diplomats arrived in the 19th and 20th centuries. These European Jews were collectively referred to as Francos in Aleppo. It was because Franco families began to send their children to private tutors or Christian schools that the community in 1869 established an Alliance Israélite Universelle school for boys; a girls' school was founded 20 years later.[48]

Although by the mid-19th century Jews were well established in Syria, they were not immune to persecution by the Muslim majority. In a horrific episode in 1840 that became known as the Damascus Affair, several Damascus Jews were accused of killing a Christian priest to use his blood for ritual purposes. A prominent member of the Aleppo Jewish community, Elias de Picciotto, the Austrian counsel, became involved as well. De Picciotto's nephew, Isaac de Picciotto, lived in Damascus and was alleged to have offered to sell some of the priest's blood to Aleppan Jews. Several of the accused were forced to confess and were imprisoned; two men died under torture, and one man was forced to apostasize to Islam. Only pressure from abroad led to the release of the falsely accused.[49]

In 1893, 10,761 Jews lived in the province of Aleppo, mostly in the city. In 1908, there were 9,335 Jews in the city of Aleppo, of a total population of 119,811. Most lived in the neighborhoods of Bahsita and Jamiliya.[50]

The Jews of Aleppo during this time were evenly distributed among the socio-economic ranks. (Damascus Jews, by contrast, were starkly divided between rich bankers and poor peddlers.) Among the community were butchers, cheese makers, soap manufacturers, burlap makers, tinsmiths, and goldsmiths. Some Jews acted as brokers, buying products from peasants and shepherds which they then traded or sold in the general market.[51]

The community's leadership was largely made up of rabbis and wealthy individuals whose positions and status were passed from father to son. The Jewish community raised money through the sale of kosher meat, by assessing taxes and fees, and through voluntary contributions.[52]

Doors of one of the six arks (*hekhalot*) built along the southern wall of the Great Synagogue. The *hekhalot* were small rooms with shelves along the walls that held the Torah scrolls. (*Courtesy of Beth Hatefutsoth, Photo Archive, Tel Aviv.*)

As noted, the borders established by the French Mandate and the subsequent realignment of Syrian territory at the close of World War I led to economic hardship for Aleppo.[53] It became increasingly difficult to earn a living in the city, and many Aleppan Jews moved away.[54] Some young men also emigrated to avoid conscription.[55] The Jewish immigrants settled in Israel, Italy, England and, increasingly, North and South America, creating a small but tightly knit Aleppan Diaspora. Those who stayed behind continued to operate in their traditional spheres as wholesale importers and exporters; as middlemen between the nomadic and urban populations; and as craftsmen, in particular as goldsmiths and silversmiths.[56]

The Great Synagogue

The structure that loomed largest in the life of Jewish Aleppo was the city's Great Synagogue, also known as the Yellow (*Al-Safra*) Synagogue, the Ancient Synagogue, and the Synagogue of Yoav ben Tseruya. Citing 2 Samuel 8:3–8, which recounts the conquest of Syria by King David and his general Yoav, an ancient Aleppan legend held that Yoav built the Great Synagogue in the 10th century B.C.E., after he conquered Aram Tsova and was granted it as a fiefdom.[57] According to the tradition, a heavenly voice assured Yoav that his temple would remain standing even after the Temple in Jerusalem was destroyed.[58]

Another ancient Aleppan tradition dates the Great Synagogue to the time of the Second Temple (5th century B.C.E. – 70 C.E.).[59] These early attributions may reflect the Aleppan Jews' attempt after the Arab conquest to justify the synagogue's existence.[60]

Based on the Byzantine architectural style of the synagogue, however, scholars believe it was built in the 5th or 6th century C.E.[61] Its earliest surviving inscription probably dates to 834.[62] When Mongols led by Hulegu Khan attacked Aleppo in 1260, the Jews huddled in the synagogue for safety and were spared. When Timur conquered Aleppo in 1400,[63] the ancient synagogue was destroyed.[64] Reconstruction of the building began in 1405 and was probably largely completed by 1418, as attested by the structure's three inscriptions dated 1405, 1415, and 1418.[65] The entire building was renovated in 1855. Until the riots of November 1947, the Great Synagogue of Aleppo may have been the oldest continually functioning synagogue in the world.

As with other buildings in the Jewish quarter, the exterior of the synagogue was simple. Its facade was of plain, white stone, and the wooden door at its entrance was not only unadorned but deliberately designed not to attract attention from passersby. Inside, however, the structure was large enough to hold hundreds of worshippers. The synagogue housed the most treasured objects of the community: antique gold and silver Torah cases; a carved wood *tevah* (the raised platform from which the Torah was read); and seven arks (*hekhalot*) constructed at different periods.[66]

From the entrance, one walked down a staircase to reach a rectangular courtyard. From the courtyard, a pathway of columns with stone arches overhead led to the main sanctuary. The edifice itself was split into two wings. The western wing, the original structure, was built in the form of three colonnaded aisles separated by rows of columns and arches. When it was rebuilt after 1400, the main entrance and exterior were scaled down in order to draw less attention to the synagogue. In the middle of the western wing was a domed *tevah*. To the left of the western wing was the entrance hall, and to the west of that the open courtyard. This courtyard had its own *tevah*, which was used in the summer, when the covered parts of the synagogue were unbearably hot.[67]

To the left of the outdoor courtyard, coming in from the main street entrance, was the eastern wing. This wing was built in the 16th century to accommodate the thousands of Jews from Spain, Portugal, and Italy arriving in Aleppo. The newcomers not only infused the synagogue with great numbers of worshippers but also introduced their own liturgy. The eastern wing was known as the *Midrash* and was accessible through a separate entrance. The Midrash contained one room for prayer and two study rooms. Along the southern wall of the Midrash, facing Jerusalem, was a small chapel with a vaulted ceiling known as the Cave of Elijah, following a tradition that the prophet had appeared there. Inside the chapel was the iron safe containing the Crown and three other prized codices:[68] a codex of the Torah and the Five Scrolls from 1351, which survived the pogrom (except for its colophon) and is now in the Ben-Zvi Institute; and two other codices of the Torah that were lost in the attacks. The existence of the four codices is attested to by Rabbi Meir Nehmad,[69] the prominent Aleppan rabbi who transcribed the Crown's dedication in the 1930s, and by the collector Elhanan Natan Adler, who saw all four on a visit to Aleppo in 1899.[70]

Aleppan Traditions Regarding the Crown

There are many Aleppan legends associated with the Crown. Perhaps the most enduring one attributes the Crown's writing to Ezra the Scribe, based on the tradition that Ezra was buried in the city of Tedef, near Aleppo. (The town, also known as Tedef al-Yahud—Arabic for "Tedef the Jewish"—is today home to the Synagogue of Ezra the Scribe.) Although there is no evidence to support this notion,[71] it is likely based on the fact that Rabbinic literature records that Ezra wrote a manuscript of the authoritative version of the Bible and that Ezra was believed to have passed through Aleppo on his return to Israel from Babylon.

The Jews of Aleppo regarded the Crown as the perfect rendering of the Torah. Even though it included vowelization and accentuation marks, they believed it to be holier than a Torah scroll; it was truly considered the community's crowning glory. Pregnant women would enter the Cave of Elijah to stand near the Crown and pray for a safe delivery; a disputant might be called forth to take an oath on its parchment; and anyone in need could enter the cave to pray near it. The letters of the Crown were thought to glow and fly out from the text.

63

The Summer Courtyard (view facing south) and its three arks. At night, lamps would hang from the criss-crossing chains that appear in the picture. (*Courtesy of Beth Hatefutsoth, Photo Archive, Tel Aviv.*)

And yet even as the people of Aleppo prayed near it and revered it, almost no one in the city ever saw it. The Aleppan community was extremely protective of, even secretive about, the Crown, and it could be viewed only in the presence of select members of the community. It was thus literally a closed book to nearly all.

Rabbi Nehmad described the Crown and the other codices this way:

> *In our city Aleppo's ancient synagogue, there are four ancient books of the Bible. They are written in square letters on parchment and some of the words are written in golden letters and various colors. On the ends of the books and on the edges of the leaves there are professional drawings of plants and flowers. These books have vowels, cantillation notes, and Masorah. The people call them "crowns" and view them as holy, more holy than a Torah scroll. The codices were placed in an ark inside the wall of an ancient cave, called the Cave of Elijah the Prophet ... A few years ago, a fire erupted in that cave and consumed the door of the ark. Miraculously, the books were saved from the flames. Therefore, the community bought an iron ark which guards against fire and placed the codices there for safekeeping.[72]*

According to Rabbi Yitzhak Shchebar, who had emigrated to Argentina from Aleppo and corresponded with President Yitzhak Ben-Zvi after the codex was returned to Israel, the Crown had been kept in the oil storage room and was saved from a fire there only by miracle. He also noted that outsiders had tried to acquire the codex. For these reasons, an iron box was designed, and the Crown and the other three ancient codices of the community were placed in it. The box was then placed on a big rock in the Cave of Elijah. The box had two locks; the key to each was given to two different wealthy and important community leaders. The box could be opened only in the presence of both key holders and under the supervision of the community's Council of Sages.[73]

According to Nehmad:

> *The codices were placed in an ark inside the wall of an ancient cave, called the Cave of Elijah the Prophet. According to legend, Elijah appeared in this place. A candle therefore constantly burns in the cave so that a person down on his luck can light an oil lamp and recount his problems in front of the ark of the codices. With tearing eyes, he kisses the ark and petitions in front of God*

*that he should be rescued from his problems. Usually there are many women
in this place — a barren woman, a bereaved woman or a woman with a sick
family member at home. She goes there and cries bitterly before the ark. She
asks for mercy from God ... Our custom here is that when someone must take
a Biblical oath in court, we take him to the ark of the codices and make him
swear while holding the codices, not a Torah scroll.*[74]

In the 1840s, Rabbi Abraham Dayan of Aleppo also recorded that the Crown
was used by those who were required to swear on the Torah. In addition, he
wrote that Elijah had appeared in the cave, and that people in trouble and
women in their ninth month of pregnancy would light candles there. Men
and women also would go to the cave on the eve of the Day of Atonement
(presumably to pray).[75] The notion of swearing on the Crown as opposed to
a Torah scroll was mentioned also by Rabbi Rafael Shlomo Laniado,[76] who
served as the Great Synagogue's rabbi in the late 18th century, and by Rabbi
Shmuel Shlomo Boyarsky, a resident of Jerusalem who attempted to obtain a
copy of the codex in the 19th century.[77]

Yitzhak Ben-Zvi pointed out that caves of Elijah are common features of
Mizrahi synagogues.[78] He believed that the traditions regarding the holiness
of the Crown were of more recent origin, perhaps beginning at some point
between 1850 and 1899, after the Crown's move to the Cave of Elijah and that,
effectively, the Aleppan Jews transferred their traditions regarding the sanctity
of the cave to the codex.[79]

Gathering Storm Clouds

By the start of the 20th century, relations between the Arab and Jewish populations of Syria took on a new character. For centuries, Arabs had seen the
Christians living in their midst as their primary threat, based on the latter's
real or imagined connection to Christian Europe's conquest of Arab lands. By
contrast, the Jews were thought of as largely harmless.[80] But with the rise of
Zionism, this perception changed. As Jewish emigration to Israel increased,
friction between Jews and Arabs throughout the Middle East rose.

In 1925, Lord Balfour's visit to Syria was marked by widespread demonstrations
because of the Balfour Declaration of 1917. Ten thousand protestors turned out

The front view of the *tevah* (pulpit) in the new Eastern Wing of the Great Synagogue. Above the reader's platform is a *"shiviti,"* a meditation aid that proclaims: "I have set (*shiviti*) God before me always." (*Courtesy of Beth Hatefutsoth, Photo Archive, Tel Aviv.*)

The rear view of the *tevah* in the new Eastern Wing of the Great Synagogue. (*Courtesy of Beth Hatefutsoth, Photo Archive, Tel Aviv.*)

in Damascus, and Balfour was forced to make a hurried exit to Beirut. The Damascus Jewish community, meanwhile, narrowly escaped attack.[81]

Tensions over the course of the next decade only mounted. On November 2, 1933, the 16th anniversary of the Balfour Declaration, the ulama of Damascus led a massive demonstration against the Jews. Demonstrators attempted to enter the city's Jewish quarter but were repulsed by police.[82]

The Syrians' support for Arabs living in Israel was based partly on their long-standing commercial ties to the community there and partly on their own ambitions for a Greater Syria. The increasing number of Jews in Israel and the rise of Jewish commerce and industrial production also posed threats to the Syrian economy. The port at Haifa competed with that of Beirut, which served the valuable Syrian transit trade, and the position of Israel as Syria's largest export market was changing.[83]

Many Syrian business people, particularly the elites who had been accustomed to moving freely between Damascus, Beirut, Jerusalem, and Jaffa, felt threatened by the developing economy of the *Yishuv,* (the Jewish community in Israel before the establishment of the state). Many of these Syrians owned land in Israel and served as absentee landlords.[85] It is thus unsurprising that Syrians were staunch supporters of the Arab Revolt of 1936–1939.[86] The revolt—which involved strikes, a boycott of Jewish production, and armed violence—found considerable media and propaganda support[87] in Syria as well as material aid and supplies of guns and fighters.[88]

The Peel Commission report of 1937, which sought to resolve the tensions by outlining the partition of the Land of Israel, ultimately set the stage for further armed confrontations. Syrian gendarmerie at the borders, with the full support of the country's interior ministry, aided Arab fighters entering Israel.[89] If the Syrians were not more active in helping the Arabs in Israel, it was only out of concern that nothing interfere with their own independence movement.

International commissions and mandates did not make Syria more favorably disposed to its Jewish population.[90] Although hostile actions were not directed primarily at the Jews of Aleppo, tensions generally increased. An organized urban revolt never materialized in Syria because the country was heavily guarded by French troops. Instead, the local Arabs turned to harassing those least able to defend themselves[91]—namely the Christian and Jewish minority populations.

Meanwhile, emigration from Syria to Israel continued. We have no statistics for Syrian Jewish emigration to Israel before 1919, when a border was established between Israel and Syria. However, the Syrian Jewish community in Jerusalem registered with the Turkish authorities in 1880, and documents refer to a synagogue called Aram Tsova in the Old City of Jerusalem in 1876. Most Syrian Jews living in Jerusalem were Aleppan.[92]

Between 1919 and 1948, 9,118 Jews left Syria and Lebanon for Israel, with almost half emigrating between 1944 and 1947, according to Jewish Agency figures.[93] This number is probably too low, however, because many traveled to Israel without British permission. Presumably more would have done so had they not been discouraged by the increasingly restrictive British immigration policy.

The looming signs of danger, of course, are easy to see in retrospect. But for the moment, the Aleppan Jewish community—if somewhat diminished in numbers—remained vital, steadfastly guarding the Crown as it had done for centuries. All that would change with the events of November 1947.

Detail of the dome of the outdoor *tevah* of the Great Synagogue of Aleppo. *(Courtesy of Beth Hatefulsoth, Photo Archive, Jerusalem.)*

4

THE QUEST TO SAVE THE CROWN

With the rise of Arab nationalism in Syria, concern over the safety of the Crown intensified. Yitzhak Ben-Zvi, later the second president of Israel, was at the forefront of efforts to bring the Crown back to Israel. He had a double interest in the Crown, as a Zionist leader and as a researcher in Jewish history with a focus on *Mizrahi* Jewish communities. In 1935, Ben-Zvi visited Aleppo, hosted by Rahmo Nehmad, a leader of the community, and he was given the honor of seeing the Crown firsthand. From that point on, his interest increased — as did his concerns. He became particularly worried when Syria fell under Vichy rule during World War II. The Baghdad Farhud (pogrom) of June 1–2, 1941, also served notice on all *Mizrahi* Jews that their days in Arab countries were numbered.[1]

Efforts to Save the Crown before the 1947 Pogrom

We have discussed the research of Umberto Cassuto, whom Ben-Zvi and Hebrew University president Judah Magnes entrusted to gain access to the

Crown in late 1943 so that they could ultimately publish a complete and correct copy of the Bible. But that same year, before Cassuto's journey, Ben-Zvi and Magnes had in fact attempted to bring the Crown itself to Jerusalem.

Ben-Zvi and Magnes understood that access to the Crown would be impeded by the Aleppan Jewish community, which had consistently demonstrated something close to paranoia when it came to the codex. Putting aside for the moment possible reasons for the Aleppan community's secretiveness, we need to understand the traditions that were passed down within the community. The Aleppan Jews believed that any individual who sold or pledged the Crown would bring a curse not only on himself or herself but also on the city's entire Jewish community. Indeed, local lore held that on the day the Crown left Aleppo, the Jewish community would be destroyed.[2] The codex contains explicit prohibitions against selling or procuring it. These clearly were added after the codex was completed. At the end of the first page was written: "Blessed be he who preserves it and cursed be he who steals it and cursed be he who sells it or uses it as collateral; it shall not be sold or redeemed forever." On the cover and at the top margin of every few leaves of text were the words "It shall not be sold or redeemed."

Given the closed and exclusionary nature of the Aleppan Jewish community, the scholars at Hebrew University believed that only an insider could gain access to the Crown. Thus Magnes suggested sending Yitzhak Shamosh, a scion of the prestigious Ibn Yichya family of Aleppo, who had been active in the city's Jewish community. A successful lawyer and an expert in Arabic literature, in 1937, Shamosh had been chosen to represent the Jewish community in the first Syrian Majlis (assembly). At around the same time, he was invited to teach modern Arabic literature at Hebrew University, and he chose to take up that appointment instead.[3] When the university broached the subject of bringing the Crown to Jerusalem, Shamosh expressed concern that removing the codex from Aleppo would hurt or even destroy the Aleppan community. In July 1943, however, he agreed to go to Aleppo.[4]

Once in the city, Shamosh approached several wealthy members of the Jewish community to gain their support for his mission but was met with resistance. He was thus forced to go before the Council of Sages (the rabbis charged with protecting the Crown) without any local backing. Shamosh left no firsthand report of his meeting with the council, but his brother later recorded the following details of his recollection: Shamosh had argued in favor of removing the Crown from Aleppo on the grounds that it was in grave danger from both the Arabs, whose hatred of the Jews had steadily grown with the rise in Zionist emigration to Israel, and the Vichy regime, which controlled Syria. Just when Shamosh thought he might convince the council, one of the sages stood up and declared, "Cursed be the one who redeems it." Shamosh responded that the Crown was the property of the entire Jewish people, that it had been placed in Aleppo in trust, and that the time had come to return it to Israel from exile. His arguments appear to have incensed the council, some of whom countered that Aleppo was not a place of exile, at least not for the Crown: "It will remain in our hands as it is written 'From now until eternity.'" The council concluded that if it were removed, the curses written on the Crown would come to pass, and the Aleppo community would be in great danger. They refused to allow the codex to be removed—not even temporarily so that a copy could be made.[5]

Shamosh's request to take the Crown to Jerusalem led to great dissent in the larger Aleppan Jewish community. Remarkably, several of Shamosh's former political colleagues even offered to steal the codex for their friend. Shamosh, who had worked with these men on various political issues, refused their offer. On his return to Jerusalem, Ben-Zvi remarked that it was a pity they had sent an honest man.[6] Indeed, although his insider status in the Aleppan community was Shamosh's greatest asset, in the end it was also his greatest weakness—he was too close to the community to act in the broader interest of securing the Crown for the Jewish people.

According to several accounts, Rahmo Nehmad, one of the leaders of the community, had been adamant in his opposition to the removal of the Crown to Jerusalem, and the other Aleppan community leaders followed his lead.[7] His opposition may have been at least partially motivated by personal reasons: Shamosh earlier had cofounded an organization that helped unseat Nehmad as the Jewish representative to the Syrian Majlis.[8]

On September 23, 1943, Shamosh was again sent to the city, accompanied by

Ari Even-Zahav, the secretary of Hebrew University. This time he did not ask to take the Crown away but only to be allowed to make a copy or notes from the codex. The rabbis refused to allow any photographing or copying, but after much negotiation, they agreed to allow the respected scholar Umberto Cassuto to examine the Crown under strict supervision.[9]

In December 1943, Cassuto arrived in Aleppo and was greeted with warmth and not a small amount of suspicion. As a Torah scholar and former chief rabbi of Florence, he was a person who commanded the respect of the Aleppan rabbis. But as a Jerusalem-based biblical scholar, Cassuto was bound to have his intentions called into question. After several days' delay, the Council of Sages finally allowed him to examine the Crown under supervision, but only after he was searched for a camera.[10] In the end, Cassuto was able to study the codex for only four days.

The opposition to Cassuto's work was unjustified, whether one considers the traditions of the Crown or the superstitions that had grown up around it. It is not known why the rabbis believed it was forbidden to take photographs of the Crown, because none of the curses they cited prohibited making copies; in fact, several complete and partial copies of the codex had been made over the centuries. Furthermore, the Crown's dedication explicitly states that any believer who wishes to examine the codex to learn about the open and closed paragraphs or the cantillation notes should be allowed to do so. As Cassuto certainly was a religious man, the Aleppan rabbis went against both the letter and the spirit of the dedication. Their stubborn refusal reflected the deeply reactionary and anti-Zionist bias among the leadership of the Aleppan community and especially its rabbis.[11]

It should be noted that among the Zionist Leaders as well, there were two different positions regarding the Crown. The academic scholars led by Magnes and Cassuto were primarily concerned with furthering understanding of the Bible and ensuring the accuracy of the text. Thus, in principle, their greatest concern was obtaining a complete and accurate copy of the Crown or at least a complete set of photographs of it. Ben-Zvi and his Zionist colleagues, on the other hand, were also driven by nationalism; they saw the Crown as a great Jewish treasure that, as the patrimony of the entire Jewish people, must return to Israel. Despite the different focuses of the two groups, however, they were united in their desire to see the Crown returned.[12]

In the end, of course, neither the Aleppans nor the Zionist leaders, whatever their motivation, won out entirely. In a few short years, the 1,000-year-old Crown of Aleppo would cease to be intact.

The Crown's Whereabouts in the Pogrom's Immediate Aftermath

In the immediate aftermath of the 1947 pogrom, many scholars, assuming the worst, believed the Crown had simply been destroyed. But in a short time, news that at least some of the Crown had survived began to trickle in from many channels across the Aleppan Jewish Diaspora. Yitzhak Ben-Zvi was tireless in his pursuit of every clue that the Crown might have indeed survived the Aleppo synagogue's pillaging. He corresponded with Aleppan Jews who had emigrated far and wide in the wake of the pogrom in an effort to determine the Crown's fate. After his death in 1963, discoveries regarding the missing pages of the codex continued to be made.

Conflicting accounts arose regarding just who was the first to find the Crown, when it was found, and the condition in which it was found. The various stories were gathered over more than four decades, both before and after the codex was ultimately returned to Israel in 1958. In this section, we summarize the at times contradictory accounts of the days immediately after the riots.

The earliest report comes from Sarah Harari, a former member of the Aleppan community, just after she emigrated to Israel. On March 5, 1948, Harari recounted that she had visited the Great Synagogue before leaving Aleppo, and that "the sexton [Asher Baghdadi] revealed to her that he had been able to save fragments of the Crown, and that they are now in safe hands."[13]

In another version of the events, Murad Faham, the man who would ultimately smuggle the Crown out of Aleppo nearly a decade later, recounted the scene he witnessed a short time after the pogrom:

> *I put my Arab clothing on, and I went out to roam around close to our house near the entrance to the Bab al Faraj neighborhood. The stores of the Jews in*

Bahsita were all burned. Near our house were large stones, and it was difficult to pass. I said to myself, "They told me the Great Synagogue was burned, I would like to see for myself." I went to the Great Synagogue, and it was still in flames. Torahs were burned, thrown on the floor. I thought, "How can I step on them, how can I pass?"

The synagogue was very large; I cannot describe to you how large it was. I went in and saw that everything was burned. I saw the large stones [of the building]; I touched them and they fell apart like cinder ash. The iron supports that held up the seats were melted like water. I entered the Cave of Elijah the Prophet; it was burned out. I looked all over for the iron safes where the codices were kept but could not find them. I went outside, and suddenly I stumbled on part of the safe, and the small iron safe was still burning. There were four iron safes in the Cave of Elijah; I could not find three of them, but I found the Crown inside the iron safe that was burning. The Crown was glittering through the side of the iron safe, and it was burning. I looked and realized that this was the Crown of Ezra the Scribe, the most important of all the codices. I took it while it was burning, I rolled it in my abayah [upper coat] in order to extinguish the fire. I went back to the Cave of Elijah and sat there. Some Muslims came and saw me. I looked like a Muslim in my [Arab] dress. They greeted me. They were collecting silver pieces from the rimonim [Torah finials] on the floor ... I knocked on the door of the sexton [of the synagogue], Asher Baghdadi. He was scared and could not come down. I called him and told him who I was. He knew me because he worked for me as an employee in the cheese works. I told him, "I am Murad Faham; open, do not be afraid." He said to me, "What do you want? I cannot come down to the synagogue." I told him, "Don't come down to the synagogue, just open [the door] for me; I want to talk to you." He opened [the door]. I told him, "This is the only codex that is left of all the codices, the Crown of Ezra the Scribe. I do not want to take the Crown home; take it and hand it over tomorrow to one of the rich leaders of the community. Siyahu Shamah has left, Rahmo Nehmad has left, Moshe Shalem has left, and only Ibrahim Efendi Cohen remains [in Aleppo]. Take the Crown and give it to him, and tell him that Murad Faham gave it to me in this condition, and all the other codices were burned."[14]

A third version of the saving of the Crown was recounted by the chief rabbi of Aleppo, Rabbi Moshe Tawil. According to this version, he and Rabbi Yitzhak Shchebar entered the synagogue, where they saw the Crown covered with ashes

The Sealed Ark in the Western Wing of the Great Synagogue. The Ten Commandments are carved in the stone decoration above the ark. (*Courtesy of Beth Hatefutsoth, Photo Archive, Tel Aviv.*)

and the iron safe broken. They took the Crown from the cave and handed it over to a Christian merchant for safekeeping.

> *The Crown was accidentally saved ... Four days after [the pogrom], we entered the Great Synagogue and we saw the ashes of all the holy books. The sexton [Asher Baghdadi] entered and told Rabbi Yitzhak Shchebar that six books were burned and everybody looked at the Crown that was dirty and wallowing in ashes. Immediately, they took the Crown and gave it to a Christian merchant for safekeeping. After four or five months they handed the book to a Jew. (I will not give his name now because he is living in Aleppo.)*

> *When it was known to me that Murad Faham intended to emigrate to Israel, I told him that "I have in my hand the Crown and I want to send it with you to the Land of Israel." Haham Rabbi Salim [Shlomo] Zefrani and his son Abraham were with me at that meeting. It was in the house of Mr. Faham, while he was packing his luggage. At the same time, a man entered with the Crown in his hand, and I handed the Crown over to Faham.[15]*

In yet another account, Rabbi Yitzhak Zefrani, son of Rabbi Salim Zefrani, claimed that his father and his brother-in-law, Rabbi Yaakov Attiyeh, saved the Crown along with three other codices, stating that they were now in the Ben-Zvi Institute in Jerusalem. "On the day of the burning of the synagogues and the houses of study, they found them on the floor of the Great Synagogue with burned and singed books. And they took them and hid them."[16] It is interesting that neither Shlomo Zefrani nor Attiyeh are known to have made such a claim themselves. Furthermore, one has to wonder about the reliability of this testimony, given that at least one part is clearly incorrect—only two of the four codices that were kept together in Aleppo were brought to Israel and are now at the Ben-Zvi Institute. (Or were all four saved that day and two misappropriated in the time between the pogrom and the Crown's reemergence in 1957? If so, why were they not all taken?)

In a 1961 letter to Alexander Dotan, a foreign ministry official posted to Rio de Janeiro who had studied the Jews of Aleppo, Yitzhak Ben-Zvi referred to some intriguing testimony from Yaakov Hazan, the treasurer of the Israelite Community Committee in Aleppo, which suggests that the Crown may have mostly survived the pogrom. Hazan was in the city during the pogroms; he departed Aleppo on January 1, 1948, for Beirut and ultimately São Paulo. According to Hazan, the sexton, Baghdadi, was safeguarding the codex. Hazan gave Baghdadi 100 Syrian pounds from the committee's treasury to obtain the Crown, which at that time was almost complete, as it was missing not more than a few millimeters of pages. Before he left Aleppo, Hazan gave the Crown to a man named Moshe Jamal. When Jamal left Aleppo about five months later, he gave it to Ibrahim Cohen.[17]

Intrigued by Ben-Zvi's letter, Dotan decided to speak with Albert (Abraham) Shayo, an Aleppan Jew who had also moved to Brazil. Shayo was the son of Ezra Shayo, who had held keys to the Crown's iron safe at the time of the pogrom. In a letter to Ben-Zvi dated January 10, 1962, Dotan reported that Shayo had confirmed Hazan's story and had added that after the fire he had gone to the Great Synagogue and found another seven or eight pages of the Crown, which he gave to Hazan. Hazan, who was present at the meeting with Dotan, said that he did not remember any such thing. Shayo insisted that he had indeed found the additional pages, but Hazan attempted to portray Shayo as being irresponsible. Dotan began to suspect that Hazan had something to hide.[18]

In still another account that came to light more than forty years after the pogrom, an Aleppan named Sam Sabbagh claimed that he was the first member of the Jewish community to enter the Great Synagogue after the attacks. He took a fragment of the Crown, which he subsequently kept laminated in his wallet as an amulet. He departed for Adana, Turkey, and soon thereafter made aliyah. In 1968, he moved to Brooklyn, New York.[19] On October 18, 1988, he was interviewed by Michael Glatzer, the academic secretary of the Ben-Zvi Institute. A photocopy of Sabbagh's fragment was made through the plastic casing and given to Glatzer, who later recounted Sabbagh's story:

> After the pogroms of November 29, 1947, when I heard that they broke into all the synagogues in Aleppo, I went to the Great Synagogue to see what had happened. I was the first one to enter the synagogue after the riots. I found that they had broken in the door.
>
> How did they manage to break an iron door? They brought experts who poured fuel and the wooden fill of the door was burned. Once the filling burned, the iron boards fell and the Arabs could enter. They opened all the Holy Arks and

took all the Torahs. They burned everything. There was not one Torah scroll left in the city. I went through the ruins until I arrived at the Cave of Elijah the Prophet. (My mother used to light memorial candles there, and I also used to light memorial candles there in memory of my parents.)

How did they open the safe in the Cave of Elijah? They turned the vault over, with the door facing down. There were three layers of tin on the back side of the safe. They cut through layer by layer in the hope of finding silver, but they found only a manuscript, a Bible codex. It was the template for writing Torah scrolls. I saw that the manuscript was damaged by fire. I saw pages that were scattered on the ground and damaged by fire. I could have taken all the parts that remained but my hands were trembling from fear and from the outrage I had seen. We thought they would come and slaughter us all. I took just one piece that was separated. The rest I left, and I told Mordechai Faham that he should take it. He took it and brought it to Israel and handed it over to Yitzhak Ben-Zvi. Asher Baghdadi was living in Aleppo then, but there was no connection between that poor wretch and the Crown.[20]

Sabbagh related that the name of God (the Tetragrammaton) was written in gold letters in the Crown of Ezra the Scribe, and that before the riots, no one in the community knew what was in the safe.[21] He was also interviewed for an Israeli television program that aired in 1993, during which he spoke of the value of the fragment as an amulet and how he believed that it had saved him when he underwent major surgery.[22] The Crown, of course, did not have any gold writing, except possibly in the first pages, which have been lost. Perhaps what Sabbagh saw was part of another codex. However, the fragment that he kept in his wallet as an amulet, although of limited value to scholars, definitely is from the Crown. Did he see one codex but take a fragment from another? Would a nonexpert, particularly someone under great stress and in a hurry, have noticed the difference?

Interviewed for the same Israeli television program, Shaul Baghdadi, son of Asher Baghdadi, the sexton, recalled going to the Great Synagogue soon after the pogrom. As his father sat in an area that had been destroyed but not burned, Asher collected pages from the Crown. He says that he retrieved most of the pages, which his father, crying, put in order. He remembered that Deuteronomy and Isaiah were missing. The pages appeared burned at their

Torah students (ca. 1947) shown in the passageway between the indoor and outdoor sections of the Western Wing of the Great Synagogue. The Sealed Ark, as noted on the Plan of the Great Synagogue (p. 53), is visible at the end of the stone passage. (*Courtesy of Beth Hatefutsoth, Photo Archive, Tel Aviv.*)

edges. During the interview, Baghdadi's narrative was not entirely clear, and he was quite emotional, as might be expected.[23]

Finally, there is still another account that came to light from the letters Ben-Zvi wrote to determine whether the Crown had survived. In a letter dated April 8, 1952, to the Sephardi chief rabbi of Israel, Rabbi Ben-Zion Meir Hai Uziel, Ben-Zvi wrote, "The main ancient and most important codex is that of Ben Asher. According to Rabbi Yitzhak Dayan, one of the dignitaries of the Aleppo faction in Tel Aviv, 'the Crown was saved by Mr. Jabar Safadiya who smuggled it to Beirut and after his death the Crown was given to his children.'"[24] In a letter to the Israeli ambassador in Rome on April 12, 1952, Ben-Zvi noted, "We have received information about the two codices. The one which is very ancient [the Crown of Aleppo] is in the hands of the Safadiya family."[25] Sometime later, he heard a different version of events, and he wrote in a letter to Yitzhak Sithon, then a leader of the Aleppan community in the United States: "It is now known to me from your relative Mr. Rafael Moshe Sathun, that it was known to him through a Jew named Mr. Yosef Atzitz, who came from Beirut, that the Crown is held by four Jews, Rabbi Moshe Mizrahi, Mr. Jack Dweck, Mr. Atzitz, and another Jew whose name he does not remember."[26]

Thus, there are at least seven stories regarding the person or persons who saved the Crown:

- Asher Baghdadi saved the Crown and handed it over to someone else (according to Sarah Harari).

- Murad Faham saved it and gave it to Asher Baghdadi for safekeeping (according to Murad Faham).

- Rabbis Tawil and Shchebar and Asher Baghdadi found it (according to Rabbi Moshe Tawil).

- Rabbis Shlomo Zefrani and Yaakov Attiyeh saved it (according to Rabbi Yitzhak Zefrani).

- Asher Baghdadi saved it (according to Yaakov Hazan).

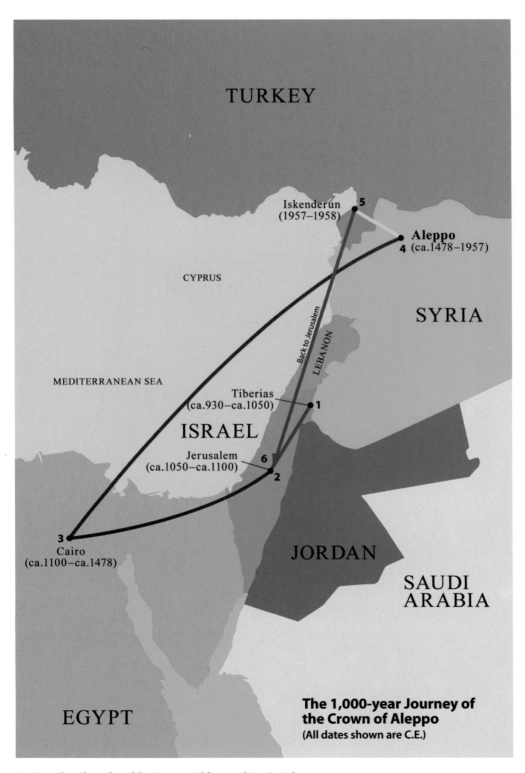

TURKEY

Iskenderun
(1957–1958)   **5**

                Aleppo
             4 (ca.1478–1957)

CYPRUS

SYRIA

Back to Jerusalem

LEBANON

MEDITERRANEAN SEA

Tiberias
(ca.930–ca.1050)   **1**

ISRAEL

Jerusalem
(ca.1050–ca.1100)   **6**

                    2

3
Cairo
(ca.1100–ca.1478)

JORDAN

SAUDI
ARABIA

**The 1,000-year Journey of
the Crown of Aleppo**
(All dates shown are C.E.)

EGYPT

Designed and produced by Steven Schloss and Boris Volunev.

Interior section of the Cave of Elijah the Prophet in the Great Synagogue of Aleppo prior to its destruction in the pogrom of 1947. Pictured is a carved metal enclosure containing jars of candles. The lighting of candles in the cave was a standard ritual to win the blessing and intercession of the Prophet Elijah. The Crown of Aleppo was kept behind iron doors in this cave. (*Courtesy of Abraham Peer, Israel.*)

A photograph of a three-column page from the Crown of Aleppo (Deuteronomy 28:17–45).
(*Courtesy of the Ben-Zvi Institute, Jerusalem.*)

A two-column page from the Crown of Aleppo (Deuteronomy 31:28–32:14). (*Courtesy of the Ben-Zvi Institute, Jerusalem.*)

A two-column page from the Crown of Aleppo (Psalms 78:38–79). (*Courtesy of the Ben-Zvi Institute, Jerusalem.*)

The final page from the Crown of Aleppo as it exists in Israel today (Song of Songs 1:12–3:11). (*Courtesy of the Ben-Zvi Institue, Jerusalem.*)

Modern day Aleppo, Syria. (*Courtesy of the Ben-Zvi Institute, Jerusalem and Harun Shamosh Imir.*)

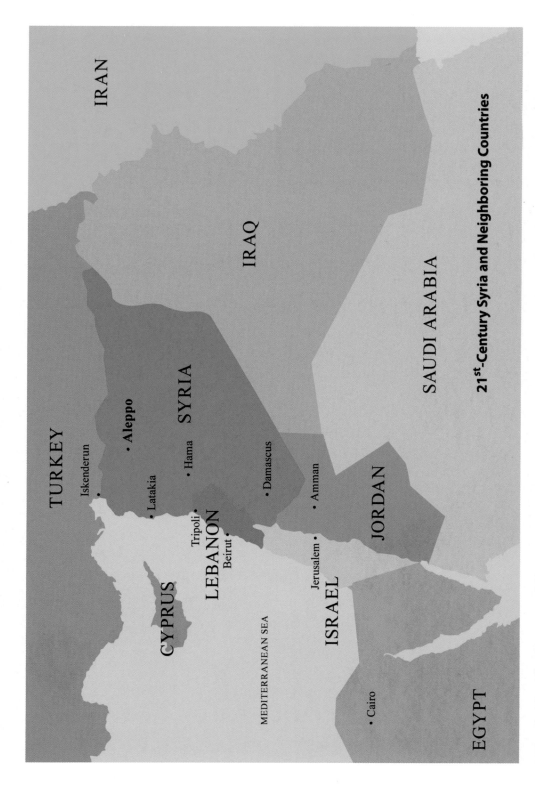

21st-Century Syria and Neighboring Countries

Designed and produced by Steven Schloss and Boris Volunev.

- Asher and Shaul Baghdadi saved it
  (according to Shaul Baghdadi).

- Jabar Safadiya saved it
  (according to Rabbi Yitzhak Dayan).

Asher Baghdadi appears in five of the seven accounts, yet there is no record of his ever having been interviewed about the Crown. Why not? Even if he did not figure so prominently in the various stories, as the last sexton of the Great Synagogue, he was an obvious subject for questioning. Was his testimony suppressed? If so, why? It also seems quite odd that most of the people rumored to have saved the Crown themselves disclaim any such role. It is almost as if no one wanted to admit that he saved the Crown. Were these men complicit in a nefarious plot? Did some of them know the truth about what happened but were afraid to say so?

Of course, it is possible that several of these stories are not in fact contradictory but actually refer to different manuscripts. Four codices were kept in the Cave of Elijah; given the confusion and chaos immediately following the pogrom, and given that most of these men had had little if any opportunity to see the codices previously, the codices simply could have been incorrectly identified.

The Search for the Crown

Soon after the initial reports of the Crown's destruction, rumors began to circulate in Israel that were, in fact, part of a ruse to keep the Crown from falling into Syrian hands. The hope that the Crown had been saved triggered renewed efforts to repatriate it to Israel.

Attempts to retrieve any surviving portions of the Crown were considered as early as March 1948, when Yitzhak Shamosh and others at Hebrew University debated the advisability of retrieving the fragments reportedly saved by Asher Baghdadi. Unable to agree on a strategy, they ultimately decided to leave the decision to Yitzhak Ben-Zvi. But any plans were soon overshadowed by rapidly shifting events. With the declaration of Israel's independence in May 1948, the new nation's border with Syria was closed for good, eliminating any chance of another mission to Aleppo.[27]

84

A portion of the Summer Courtyard of the Great Synagogue, before its destruction in 1947.
(*Courtesy of Beth Hatefutsoth, Photo Archive, Tel Aviv.*)

Meanwhile, despite all that had transpired during the pogrom, the leaders of what remained of the Aleppan Jewish community still refused to cooperate in confirming the codex's fate and salvaging what might have survived. They held firm to the belief that if the Crown left Aleppo, the dedication's curses would come true — even though by any measure the curses had already come to pass. In addition, the leaders feared repercussions if the Syrian government discovered that Jews had been hiding the Crown after insisting it had been lost. In any case, the community's refusal to reveal the fate of the codex frustrated the efforts of all those outside Aleppo who hoped to secure its safe passage.[28]

In 1953, the Sephardi chief rabbi of Israel, Ben-Zion Meir Hai Uziel, wrote a letter to community leaders in Aleppo and the Aleppan Diaspora, urging them to "do everything in [their] power to save the holy Crown from destruction and secure it in Jerusalem." He wrote that he had heard the Crown had been hidden and was being guarded by a non-Jew. He pointed out that the writers of the Crown would have wanted the codex to be safe; if the Aleppans did not secure the codex, they would be held responsible before God and the writers of the Crown. He insisted that the best and most secure place for the codex — the patrimony of the entire Jewish people — was the Land of Israel, especially now that the newly established state could protect it.[29] With this implicit lifting of the curse, the Aleppan Jews began to consider releasing the Crown. Yet it would take four more years before the community would finally let it be returned to Israel.

Yitzhak Ben-Zvi was tireless in his efforts to find the Crown. After he became president in December 1952, he used his influence to expand the search, enlisting the help of Israeli diplomats posted to cities with large Aleppan communities, including New York, Milan, Buenos Aires, and Rio de Janeiro. He prevailed on employees of the Israeli security services, representatives of many state organizations, and anyone else he thought might be able to assist him in his efforts,[30] and he undertook all this during a period of dramatic developments for the State of Israel and its leaders. (Even after a large part of the Crown was brought to Israel in 1958, Ben-Zvi continued to search for the lost pages. Upon his death on April 23, 1963, rescue efforts appear to have largely ceased, and the focus turned to preserving and researching what had been saved.)[31]

The mystery of the Crown's whereabouts in the decade after the pogrom remains unsolved. In the 1990s, a man who asked to remain anonymous to protect his family still in Aleppo claimed the Crown had been hidden in a storeroom at some point after 1947. He reported that he had seen it only briefly, and that he did not get a good look because it was hidden in a dark room. He asserted that the Crown was already unbound at that point and that its first pages were missing.[32]

Rabbi Shchebar said that he had viewed the book in Ibrahim Efendi Cohen's storeroom after the pogrom, but he insisted that very little was missing at the time. Perhaps a few pages had fallen out or been destroyed, but certainly not as many as the almost 200 pages that are missing today. Shchebar was certain that someone had tampered with the Crown sometime after the pogrom and before his departure from Aleppo in 1952.[33]

It seems most likely that the Crown remained hidden in Aleppo throughout the decade. We know that it was in Aleppo when Shchebar saw it and when it resurfaced in 1957, prior to its removal to Israel. Given the precarious position of the Jewish community in Syria and the fact that the Syrian government had an interest in obtaining the Crown, it seems unlikely that anyone would have risked removing the codex from its hiding place in the interim. It seems reasonable that parts of the Crown may have been lost in the chaotic days and weeks immediately after the pogrom, but we cannot be sure this did not happen later, as we do not know how securely the codex was kept before its return to Israel. If Shchebar's testimony is correct, large parts of the Crown must have been taken while it was hidden in Aleppo.

For now we can only speculate, because we do not know the codex's chain of possession in the decade after the pogrom. We also do not know the measures the Aleppan rabbis and community leaders took to safeguard the Crown, which had been placed in their trust. The community leaders claimed, as do their descendants, that they acted to save the Crown, but in fact no evidence of such attempts has ever been produced.[34] Whether this is because of the sensitivity of the matter or because no such attempts were made remains an unanswered question.

The Ark of the Tekiah (shofar blowing) in the Summer Courtyard. (*Courtesy of Beth Hatefutsoth, Photo Archive, Tel Aviv.*)

Murad Faham, Rescuer of the Crown

One of the more interesting characters to come in contact with the Crown in its more than 1,000-year history is Murad (Mordechai) Faham. His story deserves telling here not only because of the critical role he was to play in the codex's repatriation, but also for the light it sheds on Aleppan attitudes toward the Crown and the experience of living as a Jew in Aleppo during uncertain times.

Faham was typical of many Aleppans of his background — hardworking, shrewd, and deeply devout, but without much formal education. He was born in 1904, the son of a fairly well-off dairyman who owned sheep and camels and produced cheese and butter. His father collected sheep's milk from his own herds as well as from local Bedouin on contract for four or five cheese factories. When Faham was about 12 years old, he stopped his studies so that he could learn the family business. At about the age of 14, his father fell ill, and Faham took over running the dairy.[35]

A few years later, his father died, and Faham poured all his energy into the business. He became friendly with his Bedouin partners and wound up managing their business, acting as an honest liaison between them and the local tax collectors while refusing to accept a middleman's fee. Faham became quite successful, ultimately managing a herd of about 12,000 sheep belonging to him and his partners. He expanded the family cheese works to nine or ten factories, and solidified a reputation with local shopkeepers as a man who dealt honestly and paid on time.[36]

Faham was given the rare opportunity to see the Crown when he was a teenager. It was perhaps this episode that inclined him later in life to save the codex, despite the danger to him and his family.

> *One day, I was leaving our house, where the rabbi of the city and the head of its religious court, Haham Moshe Mizrahi, rented a room with us, near the Great Synagogue. When I reached the street I met Ibrahim Efendi, Rahmo Nehmad, and Moshe Shalem, the heads of the Israelite Community. With them were a few generals, from which country I do not know. Ibrahim Efendi was the head [of the Jewish community] of Aleppo and came from the prestigious Cohen family. He grasped my hand and told me, "Come with us."*

I asked him, "Where are you going?" and he told me, "I want to show you something you will remember all your life, something that none of the citizens of Aleppo see, not even the rabbis and the rich—only us." I went with him out of embarrassment, feeling myself out of place. We entered the Great Synagogue and went down to the Cave of Elijah. Moshe Shalem took out a key to open the iron safe, opened the ark, and then opened another iron box inside. Besides us, only the sexton of the synagogue was present. He took out three books that looked like Gemaras, bound in black leather. He took out three books and then finally a fourth one. They opened up and looked at the first book, the second and then the third. When they wanted to open the fourth one, he said to the generals, who I had discovered were French Jews, although I think one was not Jewish, "You are not allowed to touch it. I will open it myself." We washed our hands, and he told them that this is the Crown of Ezra the Scribe. He opened it. "Its script is different than the others, glittering like gold, and its paper is thinner than white paper." It was a wonder of wonders. The generals asked permission to photograph it. He said that that was forbidden; it could not be photographed, copied, transferred, taken or removed from its place. They looked through it, a Bible codex, from the beginning to the end, complete, one of the wonders of the world. Ibrahim said to me, "Look." I turned to him and he asked, "Have you ever seen anything like this? That is why I grabbed you by the hand and brought you here, because I like you. When I came by I passed many people, including neighbors of mine, and none of them was privileged to see this but you." They closed the book, returned it to its safe, and closed everything. We left the synagogue, bid each other goodbye, and each went his own way.[37]

At the age of 23, when he was not otherwise occupied by his business, Faham began helping Rabbi Moshe Mizrahi and Rabbi Shchebar distribute funds to the city's poor.[38] Increasingly, his contacts with government officials and his gregariousness placed him in the role of a "fixer" for the Jewish community. As tensions between Jews and Arabs began to rise, the Jewish community's leaders turned to him to help protect the community. In one notable incident, he successfully negotiated the cancelation of the screening of a controversial film that depicted Germans torturing and murdering a rabbi. Heedful of the Aleppan Jews' fears that the film would incite violence locally, Faham appealed to the authorities, who, in their desire to keep the peace—and in no small part also influenced by a bribe from Faham—canceled the screening.[39] In another

Ark of the Sephardi Jews (doors open) in the new Eastern Wing of the Great Synagogue. Various adorned Torah scrolls are visible in the ark. (*Courtesy of Beth Hatefutsoth, Photo Archive, Tel Aviv.*)

incident, Faham acted as a go-between to help a young Jewish girl marry her impoverished boyfriend when her father, who was adamantly opposed to the match, threatened to force her into work as a singer (considered an inappropriate job for a respectable Jewish woman). Through a combination of bribery and negotiations with local officials, Faham was able to ensure the girl's safety and help the wedding go forward.[40]

Faham and the Fate of the Crown

For about four days after the November 1947 pogrom, as Aleppan Jews were unable to leave their homes to work or buy food, Fahad provided the community with assistance and provisions. Once it was safe to go about the city, Faham used the Jewish community's funds to buy mattresses and blankets and to distribute money to those in need. Even after the initial crisis had passed, Jews were still prevented from working and forbidden to leave the city or country. The situation for Jewish women became particularly dire as they were increasingly harassed by the Arabs. Indeed, Rabbi Moshe Tawil, knowing of Faham's role in assisting the Aleppan girl whose suitor her father opposed, enlisted his help to smuggle his daughter out of Aleppo. Using his Iranian identity document, which did not list him as Jewish, Faham claimed the girl was his own daughter and was thus allowed to leave the city. He escorted her safely to Homs, near the border with Lebanon, before returning to Aleppo. He was to save the daughter of Rabbi Salim Zefrani in a similar fashion.[41]

Faham also secured Iranian identity documents for Iranian families stranded in Aleppo who wished to leave the country.[42] When he was found out—most likely through an informant—he was badly beaten and tortured by the authorities for a week. He was released after the Iranian consul in Damascus interceded, but thereafter he was repeatedly harassed by the security service and even imprisoned briefly.[43]

Faham remained in Aleppo until 1955, when he was served with an expulsion order while on holiday with his family in Damascus. Faham tried unsuccessfully to use his official contacts to have the order rescinded. Instead, he was taken in handcuffs from Damascus to Aleppo, where he was given four hours to put his affairs in order before being deported along with his family.

91

He settled his debts and was able to pack only bedding and some personal effects. He and his family were taken to the Turkish border and from there traveled to Iskenderun.[44]

Faham and his family stayed in Turkey for only 30 days. By virtue of Faham's Iranian citizenship, they were able to move next to Iran. Arriving penniless, Faham was reduced to borrowing money from several wealthy Teherani Jews. He appealed to the Iranian government to intervene with the Syrians to allow him to return and reclaim his property. The Iranian government, preferring to avoid diplomatic complications, offered to compensate him for his losses, but Faham insisted on being allowed to return. Finally, after 14 months in Iran, in 1957 Faham was granted an entry permit to return to Aleppo.[45] Before his departure, he was approached by the Israeli military attaché in Teheran, who asked him to keep his eyes open during his trip. Faham spent Passover in Iskenderun on the way back to Aleppo and then crossed the border into Syria.[46]

Once in Aleppo, Faham tried to retrieve his property, but he soon learned that his former business partners had been ordered not to cooperate with him. He was able to recover only a small amount of the funds owed him, and after about three months he prepared again to depart Aleppo.

> On the eve of my travel I went to the synagogue to bid farewell to the rabbis and my friends. Rabbi Moshe Tawil said to me, "Sit down. I want to tell you something." When I sat down next to him, he said, "I want to tell you something but I am afraid for your welfare, because the thing that I want to tell you about is very dangerous. If they catch the person doing this, he will be hanged."... I urged the rabbi to tell me. He told me, "The thing that I am referring to is the Crown of Ezra the Scribe, which came into the possession of the government after the fires. Rabbi Moshe Mizrahi asked the government to give him the Crown. The government agreed, but on condition that it never be removed from Syria. If it was removed, and the person caught, they would kill him, and anyone who was found with the Crown would be chopped to pieces. Rabbi Mizrahi agreed to this condition. He passed away, and the Crown was left in the same place, with a member of the Jewish community."[47] I told Rabbi Tawil, "Since you have told me this story, I will not drop the subject. With God's help I will take it out; do not fear for my life. For if God has decreed

that the book will be smuggled by me, it would be a great miracle that God is doing through me. And if I am caught, never mind, I have seen death more than once, and this will be the date fated for me."

The rabbi called Rabbi Salim [Shlomo] Zefrani and told him all that I had said to him, and Rabbi Zefrani said, "If he takes the responsibility to smuggle the Crown on himself, let him do it." I told Rabbi Tawil that I want to take the Crown out [of Aleppo] and not leave it in the hands of the gentiles, and I agreed that they can cut me to pieces [if they catch me], but with the help of God, I will take it out. Then the rabbi told me the Crown was in the hands of a certain person and they would tell him to bring it to my house. This person brought the Crown to our house. I placed it among our personal belongings, and we left.

At customs they wanted to search my belongings. They opened the first piece of luggage, and then I said to the customs official, "Why are you opening it?" I showed him my passport and explained to him that I had returned to Syria with the permission of the Syrian government. He answered me that he was just doing his job. We had a big argument. His supervisor came and asked what was going on. He asked my name, and I told him, "Murad Faham." He asked me, "Are you the one who was exiled two years ago?" I said yes. Then the supervisor turned to the customs clerk and told him, "They exiled him because he is a Zionist. The government seized all his property, and now he has returned. Look what gall he has. How does he dare come back without fearing for his life after they expelled him for the crime of Zionism?" I got involved in the conversation and told him, "I came back because I am innocent." Then he told the customs clerk, "Leave him alone. Do not search his luggage. Let him get out of here." That is what happened to us. The Creator of the World helped us; we were saved and we reached Israel.[48]

Before I took the Crown, I said to Rabbi Moshe Tawil, "You say I should take the Crown with me; if I reach [Israel] in peace, to whom should I give it there?" He said, "Do not give it to anyone in particular; give it to someone who seems appropriate to you, as long as you give it to a religious person." I answered, "You are not telling me to give it to anyone in particular, but rather to anyone I choose. In the future, everyone will claim that they are the owner and will sue me." He said, "Don't pay attention to anyone; you hand it over to anyone who seems appropriate it to you. Already for five years you

Mr. Murad (Mordechai) Faham and his wife Sarina in 1977. (*Courtesy of Jack Dweck and the family of Murad Faham.*)

have managed the affairs of the community. Even when they did not provide kosher meat for a month, you contacted the government and took care of the matter in a moment. You will not be capable of finding someone suitable and giving him the Crown?" I said, "What do you think about my asking Rabbi Yitzhak HaDayan?" He said, "Don't ask him; do what you see fit. I am not telling you to give it to any specific person."[49]

When we arrived in Israel, I thought about whom I should [give] the Crown to, and I asked around. I was told that there was someone named [Zalman] Shragai at the Jewish Agency, so I went to him, told him the story, and told him I want to give him the Crown. Shragai said, "Listen, Israel will get a lot of benefit and knowledge from the Crown; if it remains in my possession or yours or someone else's it will remain hidden. If you want to listen to me, give it to the president. The president will make sure that they will benefit from it—not financial benefit but academic benefit." I said to him, "Good." We went to the president. [Shragai] told him [President Ben-Zvi] that Murad Faham brought the Crown from Aleppo, and [Faham] wants to give it to [the president]. "[Faham] is the one who saved it." The president asked me which codex it was. I answered, "The Crown of Ezra the Scribe that was kept in the Cave of Elijah the Prophet in the synagogue in Aleppo. I am handing it over to you on the condition that it gets the acclaim it deserves."[50]

In the program aired by the Israel Broadcasting Authority in 1993, Sarina Faham, the widow of Murad Faham, answered questions from interviewer Rafi Citron. She recalled the following details (that at times diverge from her husband's account, which was also recorded many years after the actual events) about how they smuggled the Crown into Israel from Turkey inside a washing machine.

Sarina Faham: The Crown was wrapped in a bag like a sack. The sack was from cloth, fabric. At that time we were making cheese.

Citron: Was it tied?

Sarina Faham: No, it was not tied. I found a piece of fabric used for the cheese, and I wrapped the book.

Citron: Did you open it?

Sarina Faham: No, I did not open it. I did not see what was inside. There were some people who wrapped it up; why should I open it up to see it? I put it in the washing machine. I put a sack of sunflower seeds, onions, and some clothing on top of it.

Citron: Did you feel if there were one, two or three items in it?

Sarina Faham: There was the Crown, and something small next to it. We went to Israel. The next morning [people] came and took us straight to Haifa in order for us to open the bags and give them the Crown. My husband asked them, "Where are you from?" "We are from the Jewish Agency in order to help you out." They asked which package contained the Crown. I told them because I was the one who packed the belongings. I told them, "In this package." We opened the package in the customs office, took the Crown out, and they opened it. They saw the Crown.

Citron: Who opened it?

Sarina Faham: My husband and those who came from the Jewish Agency.

Citron: This was the first time the sack was opened?

Sarina Faham: This was the first time since Edmund [Ibrahim Efendi] Cohen [in Aleppo].

Citron: Until you got to Israel, this was the first time you opened it?

Sarina Faham: Yes, this was the first time. Then we went to [Zalman] Shragai, and we gave it to him. My husband told him, "Here it is," and that he should guard it.[51]

As we will see, Jews worldwide greeted Faham's role in smuggling the Crown to safety as an act of great heroism, but some members of the Aleppan Jewish community were upset with him for returning the Crown to Israel, and they remain so today. They believed, and still believe, the Crown to be the patrimony of the city's Jewish community and that it should have remained in their possession. Citing the curses written at the beginning of the codex, some Aleppans held the talismanic belief that if the Crown was ransomed, stolen, or destroyed, the Jewish community of Aleppo would disappear along with it.

Sadly, this prediction appeared to come to pass. After the pogrom, community leaders and other prominent figures fled, leaving behind only a few Jews in the city. But the Aleppan Jews who opposed the Crown's repatriation had confused cause and effect. They feared the community would be destroyed if

A torn page from the Crown of Aleppo (Jeremiah 31:34–32:14) after its arrival in Israel in 1958. (*Courtesy of the Ben-Zvi Institute, Jerusalem.*)

the codex were ever sold or lost, but in fact, the Crown was lost because the community was destroyed.

In large part, the Crown had been placed in danger and portions of it were lost because the Aleppan Jewish community, even before the pogrom, had not fulfilled its role as trustee of the codex. Had they done so, the Crown would have been moved to safety years before the terrifying events of 1947.

Indoor *tevah* (pulpit) in the Western Wing of the Great Synagogue of Aleppo. *(Courtesy of Beth Hatefusoth, Photo Archive, Tel Aviv.)*

5

THE DISPUTED CROWN AND ITS RESTORATION

The Crown Arrives in Israel

Given the tensions over the Aleppan Jewish community's claims to the Crown, it is unsurprising that controversy erupted immediately after Murad Faham arrived in Israel in 1958 and entrusted the codex to President Yitzhak Ben-Zvi. Three leaders of the Aleppan community in Israel, Moshe Tawil, Yom Tov Yaakov Yadid, and Salim (Shlomo) Avraham Zefrani, wrote a letter that said, in part:

> We declare that the holy Crown was sent on condition that it be handed over to the great rabbi ... Yitzhak Dayan ... specifically and not anyone else so that it may remain in the best care always ... and no Jew has permission to transfer it to the possession of others.[1]

A similar letter was signed by the three men in the name of the Religious Court of Aleppo and its branches. It was sent to Rabbi Yaakov Katzin, the rabbi of the Aleppan community in Brooklyn, and to Rabbi Yitzhak Dayan.[2] In neither of these letters was Faham named, but both indirectly accused him of having improperly transferred the Crown.

Faham recalled:

Three days after I handed the Crown over to the president, Rabbi Yitzhak Dayan and Rabbi Yitzhak Zefrani appeared at my son Ezra's house in Kfar Saba, while I was in Haifa trying to get my shipment released from customs. They asked my daughter-in-law to show them the book I brought with me. She told them that she did not have permission to burrow in my possessions and also that she was not requested by me to hand the book over to anyone. The two rabbis left and came back the next day. In the meantime Rabbi David Laniado came to visit me. He said to me, "The Creator of the Universe granted you success; I heard about the story of the Crown: tell me all about it." I told him that I took it out [of Aleppo] on the condition that I give it to someone suitable. Rabbi Laniado said to me, "In my opinion you should give it to Rabbi Yitzhak [Dayan]." At this point I felt Rabbi Laniado had been sent to get to me, and I said to him, "I have a lot of experience with these kinds of games. Have you come to bless me or to turn me around? I will give [the Crown] according to my own opinion, and especially after I asked Rabbi Tawil in Aleppo whether I should give the Crown to Rabbi Yitzhak and he answered that I should hand it over to whoever seems appropriate to me; I have already given it to the president."

As stated, Rabbi Yitzhak came the next day, and invited me to come with him so that he could show me the place designated for the Crown. We went to the synagogue of the Aleppans, near the seashore [in Tel Aviv]. There he showed me the place set aside for the Crown. And what did I see? A piece of wood that can be opened with bare hands! I said to him, "[This is] the Torah codex written by the hand of Ezra the Scribe about 2000 years ago—do you think that I will agree to keep it in a box like this that is made of wood and can be opened with ease?" He said to me, "If you agree, we will build a place of stone, the way it was in the sanctuary [the Cave of Elijah the Prophet in the Great Synagogue in Aleppo]." I told him, "In general, this place does not look suitable to my mind. It should be kept in a place like the safe of a king, and when I handed it over to the president, I was told that it would be stored in the State [of Israel]'s safe. I want a place like that. He said to me, "We will make for it a place better than the State safe." I answered him that I did not think to take it back from the president. He said, "Fine, do as you will." The president called for Rabbi Yitzhak and spoke with him. After two days, the president called me and told me that I should appoint a lawyer and told me to go to court because the Aleppan community had brought suit against me in the great court in Jerusalem. Mr. Toussia-Cohen was my lawyer.[3]

The case began in the Regional Religious Court in Jerusalem in 1958. It was argued by Sh. Mizrahi on behalf of the Aleppan rabbis. The Ben-Zvi Institute and Murad Faham were represented by Shlomo Toussia-Cohen.

Faham related:

I appeared before the court, and I told them the whole story of my life: what I used to arrange; what I used to do; the fact that I was exiled to Iran; my return to Syria; the giving of the Crown into my hands by Rabbi Tawil, who empowered me to hand the Crown over to whoever I deemed suitable; and that I gave it to the president. The trial lasted about a year—more than a year. I was subject at every session to detailed cross-examination by the Aleppan community's lawyer.

The Aleppans also pressured my son, who taught at a Talmud Torah. They said to him, "Your father has done a bad thing, he handed the Crown over to the president. We would have been enriched by it; we would have sold it for a large sum of money and distributed the money to those who needed it."

When I heard this, I became more determined not to give the Crown to the Aleppan community.

In addition to the pressure on my son, they used to bring to every session of the trial six, seven ruffians to frighten me. After seven or eight months, when I appeared in court, the chamber was packed with some 30 ruffians. The lawyer for the Aleppan community requested that I restate my testimony from the beginning to the end. I answered him that I am an ill man because of all the beatings that I suffered, my vision is poor and my health is weak, and every time you want to go over things I have said several times. What do you want from my life?! A full year and you wear me out with these court sessions. If you think I will hand over the Crown so that you can sell it, it will never happen. I was endangered in taking it out of Aleppo. I didn't try to sell it even though I'm an experienced salesman. You may be a lawyer, but I am

103

a salesman — I could have done with it as I wished, but I didn't try to get any benefit out of it and I won't let anyone else do so either. This is the last session at which I will appear." I turned to the rabbis sitting as a bet din and said to them, "Don't invite me here again to appear before you. I appeared all the time out of the respect I accord to you. As you can see with your own eyes, the chamber is packed with ruffians who try to intimidate me with all sorts of intimidating gestures."

It appears that the Aleppan community submitted to the court a letter that Rabbi Moshe Tawil sent from Aleppo, which stated that I was to hand the Crown over to Rabbi Yitzhak [Dayan]. The judges asked me what I had to say about this letter. I answered that I received the Crown in order to give it to whoever seemed to me to be suitable to receive it. Even when I asked Rabbi Tawil if I should give it to Rabbi Yitzhak [Dayan] [he said] no ... [and when I asked whether I should] ask Rabbi Yitzhak his advice — he said, "Don't ask his opinion; do what seems appropriate to you."

When we left the court, Mr. Toussia-Cohen said to me that he had read Rabbi Moshe Tawil's letter in which it said that he directed me to give the Crown to Rabbi Yitzhak. I told him that this is completely incorrect. I added that I also sent a letter to the president in which I noted that I am not handing him the Crown out of fear because he is the president, or to gain some material benefit, but so that it will be stored somewhere secure. I did not want any money for it. If anyone mentions the question of money, I will take the Crown back.

After two or three weeks, Rabbi Moshe Tawil arrived in Israel. The president had invited him to come and told him that Murad Faham spoke a lot about his actions in Aleppo ... The president asked, "Is what Murad Faham said true?" [Tawil] answered the president: "Whatever Murad Faham said is only half the story. I was in Aleppo; I did not know what was going on here; they told me to write [a letter], so this is how I wrote [the letter]."

The president asked the court to invite me and Rabbi Moshe Tawil. When I received the invitation of the court, I went to Rabbi Meir Dayan, who had been my teacher, and I asked his advice. I said to him, Rabbi Tawil has arrived in Israel and he has been invited to the court together with me. He sent a letter that stated that I should give the Crown to Rabbi Yitzhak [Dayan]. If the truth about the contents of this letter is verified, should I keep quiet or tell the truth? Rabbi [Meir] Dayan said to me that if I keep quiet I will skew the course of justice and that I should tell the truth. But, I said to him, one must consider the honor of the rabbi. He answered, the honor of the rabbi is what it is, but I should tell the truth.

At the court, I met Rabbi Tawil and I said to him, "I heard you sent a letter." Before I had finished, he answered, "It is true they tricked me; I was with the president, and I admitted to him that I never asked you to give the Crown to any specific person." The session started, and they called Rabbi Tawil first. They asked him, and he confirmed what I had said. He then left by a side door. After he left they called me, asked me for forgiveness, and announced the adjournment of the trial.[4]

· · ·

I used to meet regularly with Rabbi Tawil [after the trial] until I went to the United States, and our communications never touched on the issue of the Crown. To this day [1976], after 18 years, no one has dared to speak to me about the Crown.[5]

Although the case was suspended, it formally ended only in 1962, when the Aleppan community finally agreed to settle. According to this settlement, the Jerusalem religious court issued a writ of consecration (*shtar hekdesh*) on May 23, 1962. The primary provisions were that:

- The two codices (the Crown and a later codex known as the Small Crown, also from Aleppo) are to be kept in the Ben-Zvi Institute and never leave it.

- Any proceeds from the codices are to be given to the Aleppan community.

- A board of trustees of eight people to be convened is to have ultimate authority over the codices.[6]

The first group of trustees was as follows:

- Yitzhak Ben-Zvi, president of the State of Israel and head of the Ben-Zvi Institute, chairman

- Rabbi Yitzhak Nissim, Sephardi chief rabbi of Israel

- Rabbi Avraham Antebby, head of the Aleppan Religious Court in Jerusalem

- Meir Laniado, honorary president of the Aleppan community in Israel

- Rabbi Moshe Tawil, head of the Aleppan Yeshiva in Tel Aviv

- Rabbi Shlomo Zefrani, of the Aleppan Yeshiva in Tel Aviv

- Eliyahu Eilat, member of the board of the Ben-Zvi Institute

- Shlomo Zalman Shragai, of the Jewish Agency in Israel

President Ben-Zvi was given the power to appoint his own successor. According to the writ, upon Rabbi Nissim's death, his seat would be filled by the next Sephardi chief rabbi. (The writ apparently did not anticipate the current custom, whereby chief rabbis no longer serve until death, as had Rabbi Nissim's predecessor, Chief Rabbi Ben-Zion Meir Hai Uziel.)[7]

The Crown Gains a Permanent Home

Upon Ben-Zvi's death in 1963, the board chose Zalman Shazar, the new Israeli president, to take his seat.[8] Not surprisingly, there is no record of these early trustees having dealt with the controversy surrounding the Crown's recovery, as their primary task was preserving it.[9]

During their first meetings, the trustees debated who should have access to the Crown. The rabbis on the board wanted to limit access, whereas Ben-Zvi (and Shazar, his successor) wanted the Crown to be available to a broad audience, in the spirit of the codex's dedication and the 1962 writ of consecration.[10] In April 1965, the trustees decided to allow a facsimile of the codex to be published by the Bible Project, a joint venture of the World Union for Jewish Studies and Hebrew University.[11] This facsimile was subsequently published in 1976, and the complete surviving text is now available on the Aleppo Codex website.[12]

The actual Crown, meanwhile, continued its peripatetic journey in Jerusalem. The codex was initially kept on the Givat Ram Campus of Hebrew University in western Jerusalem. Next, it was relocated to a special safe in the attic of the Ben-Zvi Institute when the study center moved to its permanent location in the Kuzari Garden on Abravanel Street. Scholars and preservationists concerned about the Crown's condition examined the codex on December 17, 1970, and then several times subsequently. The experts recommended that it be moved

Interior view (ca. 1947) of the Western Wing of the Great Synagogue of Aleppo. (*Courtesy of Beth Hatefutsoth, Photo Archive, Tel Aviv.*)

Interior view of the Eastern Wing (the "Midrash") of the Great Synagogue. (*Courtesy of Beth Hatefutsoth, Photo Archive, Tel Aviv.*)

to a more stable environment, and on May 21, 1975, the codex was transferred to the National Library and placed in a basement repository reserved for precious manuscripts. The repository housing the Crown was then leased for the exclusive use of the Ben-Zvi Institute,[13] thereby fulfilling the requirements of the 1962 writ.

In honor of the State of Israel's 30th birthday, the Crown was publicly displayed in 1978 at the Israel Museum as part of its Manuscript, Scroll and Book Exhibition.[14] In 1986, the codex was transferred to the museum's laboratories for restoration; subsequently it was moved to the museum's Shrine of the Book,[15] where it remains on public display to the present day.

It is interesting to note that, even as the codex gained a permanent home in Jerusalem, it continued to fuel dispute and speculation. Beginning in 1995, several articles regarding the Crown appeared in Israeli newspapers, including one that cited the claim of some Hasidic Jews that the codex in the Israel Museum was a forgery. Around the same time a controversy broke out in the ultra-Orthodox world regarding the proper way to write scrolls of the Prophets. As is customary in these circles, the debate was waged by means of posters and polemic tracts. One side argued in favor of following the arrangement of open and closed sections found in the Crown, citing various sages and the fact that scrolls of Prophets written in Jerusalem after Rabbi Moshe Yehoshua Kimhi's visit to Aleppo in the 19th century used the same rules as the Crown. Others argued against the Crown's arrangement on the grounds that it goes against established tradition.[16] In December 1995, polemic broadsheets against the Crown were plastered as far away as the walls of Yeshiva University in New York City. Whether the halakhic debate was related to rumors regarding an attempted sale of part of the Crown or to a larger ideological battle regarding the Bible is unclear, but by any measure religious interest in the Crown has not abated.

The Condition of the Crown before the 1947 Pogrom

As mentioned earlier, the Crown, once in Israel, was subject to conservation efforts before it could be put on public display. But to understand how the codex came to be in its present-day form, we must first learn a bit more about the Crown's physical condition prior to 1947.

We have noted that Umberto Cassuto was the last known scholar to view the Crown in its entirety. From his notes of 1943, we know several details about how the codex was maintained in Aleppo during the first half of the 20th century. Cassuto states that it was stored in a wooden box covered with red leather. When the box was opened, it revealed that the codex's covers were fastened to the box at both ends, so that two of the box's main boards essentially served as the codex's front and back covers. Most of the fascicles (sections of the book) that made up the Crown consisted of 10 folios, but some were from 4 to 14 folios.[17] Moisture stains were already visible, and the ink on some pages was fading. Several pages were dirty and had become detached from the binding.[18] The binding itself was in very poor condition.[19]

A seven-page Masorah section appeared at the beginning of the Crown. This section contained a poem in praise of the Bible and the Hebrew language; the cantillation notes; and a prose rendering of the Masoretic grammar rules. The text of the Torah began with the second column of page eight. At the end of the Crown were 20 pages containing lists of changes and rulings regarding the Masorah. The two supplementary sections at the beginning and end of the codex contained drawings and some gold and colored letters.[20]

The Current Condition of the Crown

The Ben-Zvi Institute currently possesses 295 pages of the Crown. (In all, 294 pages were returned to Israel by Faham, and one page was returned in 1981, as will be described shortly.)[21] Each page is made of parchment and measures 26.5 centimeters wide by 33 centimeters long. Except for the books Job, Proverbs, and Psalms, which are written in two columns, and certain poems,[22] every page has three columns. Each column has 28 lines. On the three-column pages, each column is 5.5 centimeters wide and 23.5 centimeters long. On the two-column pages, each column is 9 centimeters wide and 23.5 centimeters long. The dimensions of the written area, including the spaces between the columns, are 20.5 centimeters by 23.5 centimeters.[23]

In 1981, one page of Chronicles was given to the Ben-Zvi Institute by the family of Mary Hedaya. According to Hedaya's family, her nephew had found the page on the floor of the Great Synagogue the day after the pogrom. The boy gave it to his mother, Regina Tawil, who was Hedaya's sister. When Mary Hedaya invited her sister's family to move to Brooklyn, Tawil gave Hedaya the page in thanks for helping them leave Aleppo. For years, the page remained in Hedaya's home as something of an amulet. While sitting shiva for her husband, Hedaya received a visit from the head rabbi of the Aleppan community. She showed the page to the rabbi, who recognized it and instructed her to return it to Jerusalem. When Hedaya went to Israel six years later, she left the page with her niece, Shulamit Romanov, who several months later gave it to the Ben-Zvi Institute.[24]

The original number of pages in the Crown is unknown, and there is no record of a scientific investigation of the codex's length or material composition before it was damaged. According to Ben-Zvi, there were originally 380 pages,[25] but Cassuto mentions numbers ranging from 462 to 491 pages in his notes.[26] Subsequent research strongly suggests that the complete Crown had more than 480 pages. (Yosef Ofer puts the number at 487.)[27] This roughly fits Rabbi Shchebar's description, in his letter to Yitzhak Ben-Zvi, that the codex was thicker than its approximate 25-centimeter width—almost twice as thick as it is today.[28]

One can make out the impressions of the horizontal and vertical guide lines Ben Buya'a drew before writing the text columns. In at least half the pages, the impression is deep enough to be torn into the bottom edge of the parchment. The upper outer corners of the surviving whole pages are clean and complete, but the bottom outer corners are moldy, and their edges have become rounded. The ink in some places has faded to a purplish color, and in other places it is nearly illegible. Before the extensive modern restoration of the Crown, many pages had been repaired in a makeshift manner, with paper and parchment patches. Today, the entire Crown is bound in a simple parchment cover, which was added at the Jewish National and University Library in Jerusalem after the codex arrived in Israel.[29]

On every few pages of the codex, generally in the middle of a fascicle, the words "Holy to God, it shall not be sold nor redeemed" are written in the middle of the top margin. The inscription sometimes extends across facing pages and at other times is contained on one page; sometimes the writing is cramped, and sometimes it is spread out. The exact position of each inscription depends on the available space on the page, and the ink and handwriting differ from that of the text of the Crown; clearly, these inscriptions were added after the codex was written.[30]

It is important to observe here that, despite accounts of the pogrom to the contrary, there is no fire damage to the existing complete pages of the Crown. Indeed, tests carried out by Pinhas Bergman, deputy head of the Criminal Identification Laboratory in Israel, suggest that the Crown came out of the fire stage of the pogrom unsinged and perhaps intact. Bergman's test involved creating a bound parchment book and then subjecting it to fire. When heat from the flames reached above 200°C, the parchment began to fold. Yet, significantly, there is no sign of such folding in the surviving parts of the Crown.[31] The Small Crown that was stored in the iron box with the Crown and brought to Israel also shows no sign of fire damage,[32] suggesting that neither codex was subjected to fire, at least initially.

An investigation by Bergman and Michael Maggen, a book restorer at the Israel Museum, demonstrated that the red spots that appear on many pages of the codex were caused by chromogenic bacteria.[33] An expert from the Department of Clinical Microbiology at Hadassah Medical Center further examined the Crown and identified a fungus (no longer active) that had attacked the book, especially the bottom corners of the pages, as belonging to the genus *Aspergillus*.[34]

Over the course of the 10-year effort begun in 1986 to stabilize the codex's condition and avoid any further deterioration, pieces of tape and spots of dirt were also removed from the Crown, and conservators worked to reinforce the ink where it had begun to disintegrate.[35]

Finally, we should make note of one modern-day addition to the codex that pays tribute to the man responsible for restoring it to Israel. In all the years following his heroic efforts, Murad Faham had steadfastly refused offers of money or other state assistance as a reward for his actions. He even rejected the government's idea to name a street in his honor. His one request, to which Yitzhak Ben-Zvi gladly agreed, was to have his role in the saving of the Crown noted within the book and on any future copies made of it.[36] An inscription in honor of Faham's crucial role in saving the Crown thus was attached to the front of the codex: "This Torah codex was given by the chief rabbi of Aleppo, Rabbi Moshe Tawil, and the religious judge, Rabbi Shlomo Zefrani, to Mr. Mordechai son of Ezra the Cohen Faham in 5718 [1957–1958] to take to the holy city of Jerusalem. Mr. Faham was privileged and gained merit in agreeing to risk his life in order to save it and bring it to Jerusalem, and he delivered it to the honorable President of the State [of Israel], Mr. Yitzhak Ben-Zvi.[37]

The inscription makes no mention of the controversy surrounding Faham's actions, but even so the Aleppan community apparently continued to bear a grudge toward Faham. They were able to score a small victory, with the help of the Crown's board of trustees, when the 1976 facsimile edition of the codex was published. That edition begins with text less effusive in its praise of Faham, and more favorable to Rabbi Tawil and the Aleppan Jewish community: "The Crown of Aleppo, which was for generations the apple of the eye of the Aleppan community, and which was saved by Rabbi Moshe Tawil and brought to Israel at the risk of his life by Mr. Mordechai son of Ezra Faham ... is kept now for preservation in the Ben-Zvi Institute of the Hebrew University and the Ben-Zvi Memorial."[38]

The Order of the Books in the Crown

The order of the books in the Crown appears to have followed the arrangement evident in other ancient Sephardi manuscripts, which is different from what we are accustomed to seeing in modern printed Bibles.[39] In some cases, of course, we cannot be completely certain of the original order, because the Crown is missing several consecutive books. Ancient Sephardi manuscripts typically follow the sequence Chronicles, Psalms, Job, Proverbs, Ruth, Song of Songs, Ecclesiastes, Lamentations, Esther, Daniel, and Ezra (including Nehemiah) in the Writings. The order in most printed Bibles is Psalms, Proverbs, Job, Song of Songs, Ruth, Lamentations, Ecclesiastes, Esther, Daniel, Ezra, Nehemiah, and Chronicles (usually divided artificially into books 1 and 2).[40] A comparison of the Crown's presumed order and that of modern printed Bibles is given in Table 1.

113

Table 1: Order of Biblical Books*

Modern Printed Bibles	The Crown
Genesis	[Genesis]
Exodus	[Exodus]
Leviticus	[Leviticus]
Numbers	[Numbers]
Deuteronomy	(Deuteronomy)
Joshua	Joshua
Judges	Judges
Samuel (1 and 2)	Samuel
Kings (1 and 2)	(Kings)
Isaiah	Isaiah
Jeremiah	(Jeremiah)

Ezekiel	Ezekiel
Twelve Prophets	(Twelve Prophets)†
Psalms	Chronicles
Proverbs	(Psalms)
Job	Job
Song of Songs	Proverbs
Ruth	Ruth
Lamentations	(Song of Songs)
Ecclesiastes	[Ecclesiastes]
Esther	[Lamentations]
Daniel	Esther
Ezra	Daniel
Nehemiah	Ezra‡
Chronicles (1 and 2)	

Parentheses, part missing; *square brackets,* completely missing, position assumed.
†Apparently in the same order.
‡Including Nehemiah.

The Missing Sections

The Crown's introductory section on the Masoretic grammar as well as the final sections that included the codex's dedication and Masoretic annotations were lost by the time the book reached Israel.[41]

Most of the missing sections from the biblical books of the Crown were from the beginning and end of the codex. In the Crown's current form, the first four books of the Torah are entirely missing, as is most of Deuteronomy; of the latter book, only the last six and a half chapters remain, beginning with Deuteronomy 28:17. It seems logical that the beginning and ending portions of the codex would have become detached from the core of the book in the mayhem of the riot, but it is interesting to note that the sections of Deuteronomy left intact include the bulk of the curses, which begin at 28:15. Is it possible that someone religiously learned enough to know the curses took

Torah scrolls in an open ark of the Great Synagogue. (*Courtesy of Beth Hatefutsoth, Photo Archive, Tel Aviv.*)

only the first part of the book, so as not to invoke their condemnation? And if so, might the first section have survived the 1947 pogrom, although it has yet to come to light? Certainly secular thieves and souvenir hunters would not have cared enough about the curses not to take the rest of Deuteronomy nor, indeed, have known enough to recognize what they had taken. In fact, one would have expected a secular thief to have taken the entire codex. Unless we learn more about what happened to the missing section, however, this theory must remain speculative.

The codex is missing the entire end section, from the middle of the last verse of the third chapter of Song of Songs to the end of the Bible; Ecclesiastes, Lamentations, Esther, Daniel, Ezra, and Nehemiah are completely missing.

The Crown is also missing 15 pages in five places in the middle of the codex. Three pages are missing from 2 Kings, from the middle of 2 Kings 14:21 to the middle of 18:13. Three pages are missing from Jeremiah, from the middle of 29:9 to the middle of 31:34; in addition, much of chapter 32 is missing because a large section of the following page is missing. Two sections of three and four pages, respectively, are missing from the Twelve Prophets. The first section covers from the middle of Amos 8:12 to the middle of Micah 5:1, including Obadiah and Jonah; the second is from the middle of the last verse of Zephaniah to the middle of Zechariah 9:17, including all of Haggai. Two pages are missing from Psalms, from 15:1 through 25:1. With the return of the single page from Mary Hedaya in 1981, all of Chronicles is once again complete.[42] In summary, 12 books are entirely missing and most of an additional two books are missing (see Table 2).[43]

Table 2: Missing Sections from the Crown

Book	Parts Missing
Genesis	enitre book
Exodus	entire book
Leviticus	entire book
Numbers	entire book
Deuteronomy	through mid 28:17

Joshua	
Judges	
Samuel	
Kings	3 pages missing covering 2 Kings mid 14:21–mid 18:13
Isaiah	
Jeremiah	3 pages missing: mid 29:9–mid 31:34 / also missing, due to a badly torn page: mid 32:1–4, part of 32:5, mid 32:8–mid 32:12, mid 32:14–mid 32:19, mid 32:21–32:23, parts of 32:24, and 32:25.
Ezekiel	
Twelve Prophets (Hosea, Joel, Amos, Obadiah, Jonah, Micha, Nahum, Habbakuk, Zephaniah, Haggai, Zechariah, and Malachi)	3 pages missing: Amos, mid 8:12 to the end; the entire books of Obadiah and Jonah; Michah, from the beginning through mid 5:1 / 4 pages missing: Zephaniah, part of 3:20 (the last verse); the entire book of Haggai; and Zechariah from beginning through mid 9:17
Chronicles†	
Psalms	2 pages missing, covering 15:1–25:1
Job	
Proverbs	
Ruth	
Song of Songs	from mid 3:11 to end
Ecclesiastes	entire book
Lamentations	entire book
Esther	entire book
Daniel	entire book
Ezra (including Nehemiah)	entire book

†One missing page was returned in 1981.

118

A window along the old western wall of the Great Synagogue. (*Courtesy of Beth Hatefutsoth, Photo Archive, Tel Aviv.*)

The carved wooden doors of an ark in the Great Synagogue. (*Courtesy of Beth Hatefutsoth, Photo Archive, Tel Aviv.*)

Extant Crown Pages from Photographs and a Fragment

Beyond the 295 pages of the Crown now in Israel, three pages of the codex exist in photographic form in books from the late 19th and early 20th centuries, and one page fragment was recovered from the Sabbagh family in 2007. We will look at these in turn.

William Wickes included a photograph of one page of the Crown (Genesis 26:37–27) in his 1887 book.[44] Until the Crown was returned to Israel, this was the only part of the codex most scholars had the opportunity to study. It is not clear why this particular page was photographed or under what circumstances, but it is likely to have been taken by Nissim Behar, the first principal (1882–1887) of the Alliance Israélite Universelle in Aleppo. In a letter to his superior in Paris, Behar referred to four photographs of the codex and suggested he would easily be able to have more taken. This letter correlates with Wickes's account that he received the photograph and a copy of the Masorah fascicle from Isidore Loeb, the secretary of the Alliance in Paris.[45] The mention of a copy of part of the Crown is tantalizing. Was more of the Crown copied, aside from the Masorah section to which Wickes referred?[46] And what of the other three photographs to which Behar referred? If they are photos of pages from the Torah, they are most likely the only surviving copies of those pages. A search in the archives of the Alliance, however, failed to turn up either the photographs or any copies of the codex.[47]

Another photograph, apparently taken of two codex pages, appears in a 1910 book by a missionary named Joseph Segall; it shows the Ten Commandments in Deuteronomy 4:38–6:3.[48] It is possible, though unlikely given Segall's account, that this photograph was among the four referred to by Behar.[49]

Finally, there is the fragment of Exodus that was in the possession of Sam Sabbagh. It is in poor condition and contains only parts of verses, so it has little scholarly value. It is irregular in shape and measures approximately 7 centimeters by 9 centimeters and clearly comes from a page that included Exodus chapter 8. The fragment is perforated by holes and ripped on all sides. On both sides, it is possible to see seven to eight lines from one of the columns, a few notes of the Small Masorah, and a few letters of another column. The fragment was given to the Ben-Zvi Institute in November 2007, after two years of negotiations with Sam Sabbagh's family following his death.[50]

A window along the old western wall of the Great Synagogue with a plaque above it (enlarged in inset) bearing the inscription of Eli Bar-Natan, dated 834 C.E. The inscription reads, in part: "This alcove was built by Eli Bar-Natan, the son of Mevaser ... from his labor and his money ... " *(Courtesy of Beth Hatefutsoth, Photo Archive, Tel Aviv.)*

Recovery and Reconstruction of the Text

No doubt the most gratifying turn of events would be the recovery of the missing pages of the original Crown. In the meantime, however, researchers have looked to find copies of the Crown or to reconstruct the missing text by closely analyzing the work of scholars who, over the centuries, consulted the original Crown to resolve ambiguities in the Torah text.

We know that copies of the Crown, or parts of it, existed on the basis of four separate references in the literature, although none of these copies has been located to date. In 1558–1559, Rabbi Yosef Karo (1488–1575) of Safed reportedly sent a copy of the Crown to Rabbi Moshe Isserles (1525–1572) of Cracow, Poland. The copy cost 100 ducats and included the dedication as proof of the original source of the text (as was common practice at the time). Rabbi Moshe Isserles used the copy as the basis for writing his own Torah scroll. Unfortunately, we have no further information about what happened to the copy and whether it survived World War II.[51] The 19th-century scholars William Wickes and Hermann Strack both claimed they possessed copies of the Masorah fascicles; however, neither copy can be found today.[52] Finally, Rabbi Azarya of Adumim (1511–1578) wrote in his book *Imre Bina* that he had found a manuscript of an old Torah apparently copied from the Crown.[53]

Reconstructing the Crown on the basis of earlier Torah scholars' work requires a particular sort of biblical investigation. Jordan Penkower, for example, has argued convincingly that a printed copy of the Torah currently held by the library of the Jewish Theological Seminary in New York City contains handwritten corrections and annotations that can be used to reconstruct portions of the Crown. The Torah was printed in 1490 in Hijar, Spain, just two years before the Spanish Expulsion. The annotations, which likely date to the latter half of the 16th century, state that they were made by Yishai ben R. Amram haKohen Amadi, of Amadiya, in Kurdistan. Amadi notes that he used "the text written by Ezra" to correct portions of Genesis, but that for the rest of the Torah he consulted "the text which Ben-Asher corrected." According to Penkower, this latter text is certainly the Crown; if he is correct, Amadi's notes give scholars important confirmation of the Crown's open and closed sections and the codex's distinctive treatment of Exodus 15 (the Song of the Sea). The codex probably became available to Amadi after he had already annotated Genesis, and apparently he determined that the differences between the Crown and "the text written by Ezra" did not merit his redoing the annotations for Genesis.[54]

Indeed, one happy consequence of the Crown's entensive and remarkably reliable annotations is that it is possible to use the extant Large Masorah to reconstruct at least a portion of the missing codex pages. A single example will suffice. Scholars have long disagreed over how to write the word "*daka*" ("crushed") in Deuteronomy 23:2. According to the Ashkenazi tradition and the custom of most *Mizrahi* communities, the word should be written "*daled-kaf-he.*" Yemenite scribes, however, spell it "*daled-kaf-alef.*" Although the codex page containing this part of Deuteronomy was lost in the pogrom, the Crown's Large Masorah on Psalms 90:3 indicates that there are two other places in the Bible where "*daka*" is spelled "*daled-kaf-alef*"—Isaiah 57:15 and Deuteronomy 23:2. Thus we know that the Yemenite tradition follows that of the Crown. This also coincides with Cassuto's observations and the responses of Rabbi Mensashe Sithon of Aleppo, the author of a list of notes regarding the writing of this word that was included with the Crown, a copy of which was preserved by Cassuto.[55]

Rabbi Sithon, who had lived in Aleppo in the mid-19th century, was in fact a widely respected local authority regarding questions of the Crown's vocalization, spelling, and grammar. In the 1850s, Sithon had provided assistance to Yaakov Sapir, an Ashkenazi rabbi living in Jerusalem, who had asked the Aleppan rabbi to determine the Crown's treatment of orthography, vocalization, and accentuation in more than 500 instances throughout the Torah, the *haftarot,* and the Five Scrolls. Sithon annotated the list with the answers to each case and returned them to Sapir.[56] Thereafter, the list was copied by subsequent scholars, so that today we can study Sithon's responses to at least partially reconstruct the Crown's treatment of those sections of the Bible.[57]

Similar information can be gleaned from the work of the scribe Rabbi Shalom Shakhna Yellin (1790–1874), of Skidel, Lithuania. Yellin was greatly interested in questions of Masorah and determining the correct text of the Bible. Traveling to Israel in 1855, Yellin examined Torah scrolls in the communities through

123

Interior passageway of the new Eastern Wing of the Great Synagogue. Light enters from the open courtyard to the right. (*Courtesy of Beth Hatefutsoth, Photo Archive, Tel Aviv.*)

which he passed. Once in Jerusalem, he hoped to travel to Aleppo to study the Crown, but he ultimately was not able to make the journey. In his stead, he sent his son-in-law, Rabbi Moshe Yehoshua Kimhi. Yellin gave Kimhi a Bible which he had annotated with questions requiring clarification. Kimhi arrived in Aleppo and was given access to the codex. He recorded answers to each of Yellin's queries according to the Crown's text, noting them in Yellin's Bible.

Although the information was subsequently disseminated among scholars of the time, for many years Yellin's Bible could not be located. Indeed, no sign of the Bible appeared for nearly a century. In 1987, however, the missing text was uncovered in an old house in Kiryat Moshe, Jerusalem that was scheduled to be razed. Just before the home was destroyed, some of the old books and documents stored in the attic were retrieved. One of the books was a small, worn copy of the Bible with tiny handwritten notes in the margins that was later confirmed as Yellin's.[58]

Scholars will no doubt continue to extrapolate the Crown's missing content from the archival record and uncover the manner in which the Crown treated questions of orthography, vocalization, and accentuation. In the interim we can hope too that the lost pages of the codex may be rediscovered.

Doors of an ark located along the southern wall of the Outdoor Courtyard of the Great Synagogue of Aleppo. (Courtesy of Beth Hatefutsoth, Photo Archive, Tel Aviv.)

6

EPILOGUE: THE FUTURE OF THE CROWN

More than 60 years after the pogrom in Aleppo, a firm chronology of the Crown's whereabouts between 1947 and 1957 and the fate of two-fifths of the manuscript remain shrouded in a thick and seemingly impenetrable mist. As of this writing, indeed, very little is certain: The codex appears to have been damaged during the pogrom, but probably not by fire. The remaining pages show few signs of tearing. At least part of the Crown was saved and hidden, ultimately making its way back to Israel through the efforts of Murad Faham.

All else remains conjecture. We do not know at what point the missing sections were separated from the codex; whether they were destroyed, lost, or stolen; or if they are still hidden. The roles and identities of the people who may have handled the Crown after the pogrom are unknown. Even the basic sequence of events since November 1947 remains unclear and in dispute, and virtually everyone who came into contact with the codex after the pogrom must be suspected of knowing more than they have revealed to date. There are now more unanswered questions than clearly established facts.

The Fate of the Missing Pages

What we do know about the missing parts of the Crown is a mix of facts and speculation. Large sections are missing from the beginning and end of the codex, with pages also missing from several places in the middle. The fact that entire books of the Torah and large parts of several books are missing suggests that the Crown was dismantled purposefully but without care, perhaps during a hasty, opportunistic theft. As noted earlier, the section in Deuteronomy containing the curses was left virtually intact,[1] as if the person or persons who took the rest of the Torah portions feared the implications of possessing that section of Deuteronomy.

It is of course quite possible that all of the missing pages have now been lost or destroyed. Certainly there was enough chaos and confusion during and after the pogrom, and the Crown remained in undocumented and perhaps unscrupulous hands for a full decade after the events of 1947. But many people knew of the codex's value or at least had some idea of its importance. Thus it is quite possible that some of the Crown's missing pages have survived.

Any number of lost pages may be in the hands of members of the Aleppan Jewish community who may consider the pages or fragments in their possession as *kamiyahs,* or amulets, as Sam Sabbagh did. Or they may yet feel that the Crown remains the patrimony of their community and thus believe they have the right to possess a part of it. Indeed, as we have seen, the Crown was the pride of the Aleppan Jews, and it had long served as a vital source of the community's identity and traditions.[2] The community's desire to reassert its control over the Crown spawned the controversy surrounding its return to Israel and explains why some Aleppan Jews might be reluctant to disclose the location of the missing pages to this day.

We have some tantalizing clues that parts of the Crown, perhaps even large parts, survive. In 1993, Shimon Savir, a former Israeli police chief, traveled to London to interview Shlomo Moussaieff, a wealthy jeweler and one of the largest private collectors of Judaica and biblical antiquities today.

The Crown on its arrival in Israel, 1958. The words "Torah Crown" *Keter Torah* appear on the cover along with the number "1" to distinguish it from a second small codex that was brought to Israel at the same time. (*Courtesy of the Ben-Zvi Institute, Jerusalem.*)

Moussaieff recounted that he had attended a Judaica exhibit and auction in Jerusalem in the late 1980s. At that time, two men dressed in Hasidic attire visited him in his room at the Hilton Hotel. (Moussaieff believed they were indeed Hasidim, not merely men disguised in Hasidic garb.) The men told him they had something he might be interested in acquiring. They claimed the item was worth $1 million, but they would sell it to Moussaieff for $750,000. Moussaieff asked to see the item and was taken to their suite in the same hotel. Once there, the men opened a briefcase, and Moussaieff could see a stack of 70 to 100 manuscript pages, with a distinctive square script twice the size of the letters in a typical Torah scroll but with diacritic marks. The letters and marks were written in black ink that had turned slightly reddish, and he described the whole effect as appearing to make the letters dance.

Savir asked Moussaieff to compare what he had seen with another text—without revealing to him that the second text was in fact a copy of the Crown. Moussaieff said he was certain they were written by the same hand. Moussaieff had not pursued the purchase because he felt there was something suspicious about the men, but he subsequently regretted his decision.[3]

A Mandate to Restore the Crown

Despite hints that the missing pages may still exist, the Israeli government, to the best of our knowledge, has not taken much action since the 1960s to discover what happened to the Crown. Certainly, Israel was fighting for survival in its early years of nationhood, but given the Crown's importance and President Ben-Zvi's personal role in retrieving it, the government's lack of involvement is surprising. It is also possible that the Israeli government investigated the whereabouts of the missing pages and chose for whatever reason not to make its discoveries public. Indeed, in 1992, one of the authors questioned a senior member of the Mossad about what had happened to the missing parts of the Crown. The agent replied, "Leave the subject alone. You don't want to know. It's a very dirty story."[4]

If it has not done so, the State of Israel should pursue the matter. The Crown is a document of national and religious importance. As the patrimony of the entire Jewish people, it is the responsibility of the State of Israel.

Similarly, the Aleppan Jewish community has an obligation to fulfill its responsibility regarding the Crown by doing everything it can to recover any missing pages that may have survived. The Aleppans held the Crown in a sacred trust for more than 500 years. They must now fulfill their duty as trustees by bringing the rest of the Crown home to Israel and to the rest of the Jewish people.

We may never discover the truth about what happened to the Crown, but as long as it is possible to retrieve even some of the missing pages, the greatest possible efforts must be made to save this most important of biblical texts.

132

The Chief Sephardi Rabbi (*Hakham*) Ben-Zion Meir Hai Uziel, in 1953. (*Courtesy of the Ben-Zvi Institute, Jerusalem.*)

President Ben-Zvi, studying the Crown on its arrival in Israel in 1958. (*Courtesy of the Hebrew University, David Rubinger, photographer.*)

The Crown, open, on its arrival in Israel, 1958. (*Courtesy of the Ben-Zvi Institute, Jerusalem.*)

Professor Abraham Harman, President of the Hebrew University, awards the first facsimile of the Crown of Aleppo to Murad (Mordechai) Faham in 1976. From left to right: Murad Faham, Mr. Abraham Peer (Faham's son), and President Abraham Harman. An unidentified woman appears on the right. (*Courtesy of the Hebrew University, Shlomo Mercus, photographer.*)

135

נשיא מדינת ישראל

ירושלים, יב' כסליו תש״ך
13 בדצמבר 1959

לכבוד
מר מרדכי בן עזרא פחם,
בני ברק.

מר פחם הנכבד,

אני רואה לנכון להביע לך בזה את תודתי
האישית על מאמציך המוצלחים, אשר השעתם בהצלת שני הכתרים
היקרים, שהאחד מהם הוא הכתר של בן־אשר, שהיו שמורים
במערת אליהו הנביא בבית הכנסת הקדמון בארם־צובא.

אני יודע להעריך את העמל ואת מסירות הנפש
שלך בהצלת הכתרים, שהיתה כרוכה בסכנת נפשות, והקב״ה עזר
לך בדרכך. כל זאת עשית שלא על מנת לקבל פרס או תמורה כל
שהיא ומסרה את שני הכתרים לידי באמצעות מר ש. ז. שרגאי,
ויהיה מכתבי זה לך לעדות שהכתרים נמסרו לידי.

כורים

יצחק בן־צבי

A letter of an appreciation and its English translation (see right-hand page), from President Ben-Zvi to Murad (Mordechai) Faham for his great efforts in saving the Crown. (*Courtesy of the Ben-Zvi Institute, Jerusalem.*)

136

President of the State of Israel

Jerusalem, 12th of Kislev 5720
13th December 1959

To
Mr. Mordechai Ben Ezra Faham
Bnei Brak

Dear Mr. Faham:

I deem it proper to hereby express to you my personal thanks for your successful efforts, which you have invested in rescuing the two precious crowns, one of which is the Crown of Ben-Asher, which were safeguarded in the cave of the Prophet Elijah in the ancient synagogue in Aleppo.

I appreciate your toil and self sacrifice in rescuing the Crowns, which involved mortal danger. God assisted you in your endeavor. All of this you did without any expectation of reward or compensation of any kind, and you delivered the two Crowns into my hands through the intercession of Mr. S. Z. Shragai. Let this letter of mine be evidence for you that the Crowns were delivered to me.

With felicitation,
Yitzhak Ben-Zvi

כתר תורה זה נמסר ע״י הרב הראשי בחלב
רבי משה טוויל והדיין ר׳ שלמה זעפראני
למר מרדכי בן עזרא הכהן פחאם
בשנת תשי״ח
על מנת להעלותו לירושלים עיר הקודש

זכה מר פחאם ונתגלגלה זכות זאת על־ידו
בהסכימו לחרף נפשו כדי להצילו
ולהביאו לירושלים

ומסרו לידי
כב׳ נשיא המדינה מר יצחק בן־צבי

A testimonial and its English translation (see right-hand page), honoring Murad (Mordechai) Faham that appeared in the first facsimile edition of the Crown in 1976. (*Courtesy of the Ben-Zvi Institute, Jerusalem.*)

The testimonial included with the Crown of Aleppo

This Torah codex was given by the chief rabbi of Aleppo,

Rabbi Moshe Tawil,

and the religious judge, Rabbi Shlomo Zefrani,

to Mr. Mordechai son of Ezra

the Cohen Faham in 5718 [1957–1958]

to take to the holy city of Jerusalem.

Mr. Faham was privileged and gained merit

in agreeing to risk his life in order to save it

and bring it to Jerusalem, and he delivered it

to the Honorable President of the State [of Israel],

Mr. Yitzhak Ben-Zvi.

Chapter 1

1. Hitti, *History of Syria,* pp. 66–68.

2. Astor, Borenstein-Makovetsky, Cohen and Shiloah, "Aleppo," p. 613.

3. Bostom, ed., T*he Legacy of Jihad: Islamic Holy War and the Fate of Non-Muslims,* p. 32.

4. Johnson, *All Honourable Men: The Social Origins of War in Lebanon,* p. 150.

5. Khoury, *Syria and the French Mandate: The Politics of Arab Nationalism, 1920–1945,* p. 475.

6. Rabin, "Interview with Murad Faham," p. 16.

7. Khoury, *Syria and the French Mandate: The Politics of Arab Nationalism, 1920–1945,* pp. 553–554; see also *Palestine Royal Commission Report.*

8. Browne, "Jews in Grave Danger in all Moslem Lands," p. E4.

9. Porath, "Letter."

10. Haron, *Palestine and the Anglo-American Connection,* p. 88; and Laqueur, *The History of Zionism,* p. 582.

11. Haron, *Palestine and the Anglo-American Connection,* p. 88.

12. Rahel Yanait Ben-Zvi, *BiShlihut laLevanon uleSuriya,* pp. 34–35.

13. Sutton and Kirzner, eds., *Aleppo: City of Scholars,* p. 28.

14. Dogs are considered unclean in Islam, so calling someone a dog is a particularly grave insult; Bosworth et al., eds., *Encyclopaedia of Islam,* pp. 4:489b–490.

15. Tawil, "Interview," p. 3.

16. Ibid.

17. Rabin, "Interview with Murad Faham," pp. 16–17.

18. Ibid., pp. 18–19.

19. Ibid.

20. Pipes, *Greater Syria: The History of an Ambition,* p. 57.

21. See, e.g., Rabin, "Interview with Murad Faham."

22. Zenner, *A Global Community: The Jews from Aleppo, Syria,* p. 61.

23. The Hebrew Bible or TANAKH consists of the 24 books that are included in the Jewish biblical canon. All references to the Bible in this book are to the Hebrew Bible.

24. Shamosh, *HaKeter: Sipuro shel Keter Aram Tsova,* pp. 10–11.

25. Umberto Cassuto, "HaTanakh shel Haleb."

Chapter 2

1. See Allony, *"HaSefer uMelekhet haSefer beErets Yisrael Bime haBenayim,"* p. 2.

2. Glatzer, *"Melekhet haSefer beKeter Aram Tsova veHashlakhoteha,"* pp. 260–261.

3. Glatzer, "The Book of Books — From Codex to Scroll and into Print," pp. 68–69.

4. Assaf and Mayer, eds., "Tiberias," p. 1131.

5. Ibid., p. 1132.

6. Ibid., p. 1131.

7. Dudman, *Tiberias,* p. 80.

8. Allony, *"HaSefer uMelekhet haSefer beErets Yisrael Bime haBenayim,"* pp. 2–3.

9. Ibid., pp. 2, 20–21.

10. Assaf and Mayer, eds., "Tiberias," p. 1133.

11. Adler, *The Itinerary of Benjamin of Tudela,* p. 44.

12. Allony, *"Sefer haTora vehaMitshaf beKriyat haTora beTsibur beAdat haRabanim uveAdat haKaraim,"* p. 332.

13. Allony, *"HaSefer uMlekhet haSefer beErets Yisrael Bime haBenayim,"* p. 3.

14. Aron Dotan, "Masorah," p. 625.

15. See, e.g., Babylonian Talmud, *Gittin* 60a.

16. Aron Dotan, "Masorah," p. 625.

17. Goshen-Gottstein, "The Aleppo Codex and the Rise of the Masoretic Bible Text," pp. 155–156.

18. Aron Dotan, "Masorah," pp. 629, 633.

19. Ibid., pp. 624–630.

20. Ofer, "The History and Authority of the Aleppo Codex," pp. 32–33.

21. Ben-Hayyim "Ben-Asher, Aaron Ben Moses" p. 320.

22. See generally Morag, "Pronunciations of Hebrew."

23. Aron Dotan, "Masorah," p. 620.

24. Shamosh, *HaKeter: Sipuro shel Keter Aram Tsova*, p. 23.

25. Sarna, et al., "Bible," p. 587.

26. Shamosh, *HaKeter: Sipuro shel Keter Aram Tsova*, p. 23.

27. Allony, *"HaSefer uMelekhet haSefer beErets Yisrael Bime haBenayim,"* pp. 8, 14.

28. Yitzhak Ben-Zvi, *"'Keter haTora' shel Ben-Asher,"* p. 2.

29. Aron Dotan, "Ben-Asher, Moses," p. 321.

30. There is no reason to believe that the Crown did not originally include a colophon, but it was lost long ago. Some have argued that the original colophon was not lost but deliberately hidden or destroyed; see Szyszman, *"La famille des massorètes karaïtes ben Asher et le Codex Alepensis,"* p. 547.

31. See Allony, *"Iyunim beKetav haHakdasha shel Keter Aram Tsova."*

32. Yitzhak Ben-Zvi, *"'Keter haTora' shel Ben-Asher,"* p. 2. Another copy of the dedication was made by Harkavy (1835–1919), who saw the Crown four times. In his 1943 trip to Aleppo, Cassuto compared the extant versions of the dedication to the original; Ofer, *"Keter Aram Tsova leOr Reshimotav shel M. D. Cassuto,"* p. 287.

33. Nehmad, *"Maamar Hakira al haKeter haYakar haNikra Keter Aram Tsova,"* p. 3.

34. Ibid., p. 6; see also Ofer, *"Keter Aram Tsova leOr Reshimotav shel M. D. Cassuto,"* p. 287, which includes and discusses the notes made by Cassuto regarding the dedication when he visited Aleppo in 1943.

35. See, e.g., Grätz, *"Die beiden Ben-Ascher und die Masora."*

36. See, e.g., Kahle, *Masoreten des Westens,* pp. 1–14.

37. See Wickes, *A Treatise on the Accentuation of the Twenty-One So-Called Prose Books of the Old Testament.*

38. See, e.g., Allony, *"Rambam, Ben Asher uBen Buyaa Meshamshim Keter Aram Tsova"*; and Yeivin, *"Keter Aram Tsova, Nikudo uTeamav."*

39. Ofer, "The History and Authority of the Aleppo Codex," pp. 36–37. However, the separation into sections and the writing of the songs in the two codices are not the same, suggesting the importance of Ben Asher's involvement; see Shamosh, *HaKeter: Sipuro shel Keter Aram Tsova,* pp. 16, 102–103.

40. See Yitzhak Ben-Zvi, *"'Keter haTora' shel Ben-Asher,"* pp. 2–3.

41. Ofer, "The History and Authority of the Aleppo Codex," p. 36.

42. St. Petersburg, Firkovich II, Ms. 39.

43. *Mishneh Torah,* Sefer Ahavah, Hilkhot Sefer Torah, 8:4.

44. Yitzhak Ben-Zvi, *"'Keter haTora' shel Ben-Asher,"* p. 5.

45. Ofer, "The History and Authority of the Aleppo Codex," pp. 37–38.

46. See, for example, Grätz, *"Die beiden Ben-Ascher und die Masora,"* p. 52 ff.

47. See, e.g., Wickes, *A Treatise on the Accentuation of the Twenty-One So-Called Prose Books of the Old Testament,* vii ff.

48. Abrahams and Roth, "Cassuto, Umberto," p. 510.

49. See Ben-Sasson, "The Bible and the Hebrew University of Jerusalem," p. 4.

50. Sarna et al., "Bible," p. 587.

51. Letter from Umberto Cassuto to Paul Kahle, December 27, 1947, reprinted in Kahle, "The new Hebrew Bible," p. 418.

52. Umberto Cassuto, *"HaTanakh shel Haleb."*

53. Oxford Huntington 80, which was in Aleppo for an extended period.

54. Goshen-Gottstein, "The Authenticity of the Aleppo Codex," 29 ff.; and Ofer, "The History and Authority of the Aleppo Codex," pp. 38–39.

55. Shamosh, *HaKeter: Sipuro shel Keter Aram Tsova*, pp. 14–15, 165–174.

56. Hofman, "Karaites," p. 787.

57. Ibid., p. 786.

58. For example, the Karaites start the new month on the basis of actual sightings of the new moon, and they started the spring season based on the growth of freshly ripened barley. These and other calendrical rules mean that the Karaites celebrate the holidays at different times of the year than the majority of Jews, who long ago began following a pre-set calendar; Hofman, "Karaites," p. 798. In some cases, the Karaite interpretation of the Bible is stricter than the Rabbanite. For example, the Karaite prohibition against working on Shabbat is defined more broadly; Hofman, "Karaites," p. 798. Similarly, the Karaites reject the minimum quantities of forbidden items that can make foods unkosher on the grounds that any amount of a forbidden ingredient, such as pork, makes a food prohibited; Hofman, "Karaites," pp. 788, 799. In other cases, the Karaite reading of the Bible leads them to adopt more lenient rules. For example: Karaites hold that eating fowl with milk or butter is not forbidden, based on a literal reading of the prohibition in Exodus 23:19 and 34:26, and in Deuteronomy 14:21 against boiling a kid in its mother's milk; Hofman, "Karaites," p. 799.

59. Allony, *"HaSefer uMelekhet haSefer beErets Yisrael Bime haBenayim,"* pp. 3–4, 23; and Allony, *"Sefer haTora vehaMitshaf beKriyat haTora beTsibur beAdat haRabanim uveAdat haKaraim."*

60. Nehmad, *"Maamar Hakira al haKeter haYakar haNikra Keter Aram Tsova,"* p. 8.

61. Hofman, "Karaites," p. 789.

62. Ibid.

63. Ibid., pp. 789–790.

64. Nehmad, *"Maamar Hakira al haKeter haYakar haNikra Keter Aram Tsova,"* p. 8.

65. Ibid., p. 14.

66. Ben-Hayyim, "Ben-Asher, Aaron Ben Moses," pp. 319–320.

67. Szyszman, *"La famille des massorètes karaïtes ben Asher et le Codex Alepensis,"* pp. 540, 543.

68. Ibid., pp. 544–545.

69. Ibid., pp. 549–550.

70. Ben-Hayyim, "Ben-Asher, Aaron Ben Moses," p. 319.

71. Szyszman, *"La famille des massorètes karaïtes ben Asher et le Codex Alepensis,"* pp. 539 ff.

72. Ibid., p. 539.

73. Ibid., pp. 533–534.

74. Yitzhak Ben-Zvi, *"'Keter haTora' shel Ben-Asher,"* p. 3.

75. Hofman, "Karaites," p. 792.

76. Ibid., p. 793.

77. Ibid.

78. Ibid.

79. Ben-Shammai, "Firkovich, Abraham," p. 44.

80. Ibid.

81. Ibid.

82. Ibid.

83. Elkin and Ben-Sasson, *"Avraham Firkovich uGenizat Kahir,"* pp. 60–61.

84. Ibid.

85. Yitzhak Ben-Zvi, "'*Keter haTora*' shel Ben-Asher," p. 7.

86. Ibid., pp. 12–13.

87. See Ben-Shammai, "Firkovich, Abraham," p. 44.

88. Shamosh, *HaKeter: Sipuro shel Keter Aram Tsova*, p. 17.

89. Ofer, "The Jerusalem Crown and Its Editorial Principles," p. 58.

90. Goshen-Gottstein, "The Aleppo Codex and the Rise of the Masoretic Bible Text," p. 150.

91. Ibid., p. 148.

92. Malachi Beit-Arié, director of the National Archives of Israel, has noted that the Russian National Library in St. Petersburg has 2,500 codices of all or part of the TANAKH dating before 1100; see Sanders, "Understanding the Development of the Biblical Text." Although the status of the Aleppo Codex seems quite secure, definitive statements about it and the Leningrad Codex must await further research of that collection.

93. Goshen-Gottstein, "The Aleppo Codex and the Rise of the Masoretic Bible Text," p. 148.

94. Ofer, "The History and Authority of the Aleppo Codex," p. 36.

95. See Shamosh, *HaKeter: Sipuro shel Keter Aram Tsova*, p. 16.

96. Goshen-Gottstein, "The Aleppo Codex and the Rise of the Masoretic Bible Text," p. 151.

97. Ibid., p. 154.

98. Ofer, "The History and Authority of the Aleppo Codex," pp. 34–35.

99. Goshen-Gottstein, "The Aleppo Codex and the Rise of the Masoretic Bible Text," p. 149.

100. Breuer, *Keter Aram Tsova vehaNusah haMekubal shel haMikra*.

Chapter 3

1. Gil, *A History of Palestine, 634–1099*, p. 617.

2. Abramsky and Gibson, "Jerusalem," p. 154.

3. Ibid., p. 157.

4. Adler, ed. and trans., *The Itinerary of Benjamin of Tudela*, p. 22.

5. See Nehmad, *"Maamar Hakira al haKeter haYakar haNikra Keter Aram Tsova."* According to Ben-Zvi, we know that Hezekiah, one of the two Karaite princes to whom the Crown was entrusted, was still alive in 1064; Yitzhak Ben-Zvi, *"'Keter haTora' shel Ben Asher,"* p. 4.

6. Ben-Zvi argued that the codex was carried to Egypt as part of the Seljuk booty after the sack of Jerusalem in 1071; Yitzhak Ben-Zvi, *"'Keter haTora' shel Ben Asher,"* p. 4. Kahle, in *Masoreten des Westens,* pp. 9–11, argued that it was taken by the Crusaders in 1099 to Egypt and returned to Jerusalem in 1105.

7. Nehmad, *"Maamar Hakira al haKeter haYakar haNikra Keter Aram Tsova,"* pp. 5–6.

8. Holt et al., eds., *The Central Islamic Lands,* pp. 184–185.

9. See Jeremiah 43:7.

10. Ashtor, Yaari and Cohen, "Cairo," pp. 342–343.

11. Ben-Sasson, "Genizah, Cairo," p. 478.

12. Goitein, *HaYishuv beErets Yisrael beReshit haIslam ubeTekufat haTsalbanim leOr Kitve haGeniza,* pp. 231–232.

13. Lewis, *The Jews of Islam,* p. 52.

14. Yitzhak Ben-Zvi, *"'Keter haTora' shel Ben Asher,"* p. 5.

15. Ibid., p.5.

16. Shamosh, *HaKeter: Sipuro shel Keter Aram Tsova,* p. 98.

17. Aron Dotan, *"HaOmnam Haya Ben Asher Karai?"*

18. Yitzhak Ben-Zvi, *"'Keter haTora' shel Ben Asher,"* p. 5.

19. Ibid., pp. 5–6.

20. Russell, *The Natural History of Aleppo*, pp. 59, 399.

21. Shamosh, *HaKeter: Sipuro shel Keter Aram Tsova*, p. 78.

22. Ibid, pp. 78–80.

23. Szyszman, *"La famille des massorètes karaïtes ben Asher et le Codex Alepensis,"* p. 534.

24. Bosworth et al., eds., *The Encyclopaedia of Islam*, p. 261.

25. Ibid., p. 261.

26. Ibid., pp. 261–262.

27. Ibid., p. 262.

28. Zenner, *A Global Community: The Jews from Aleppo, Syria*, p. 33.

29. Benisch, ed., *The Travels of Rabbi Petachia of Ratisbon*, p. 53.

30. Holt et al., eds., *The Central Islamic Lands*, p. 212.

31. Ashtor, Borenstein-Makovetsky and Cohen, "Aleppo," p. 614.

32. Lapidus, *Muslim Cities in the Later Middle Ages*, p. 79.

33. Ibid., p. 33.

34. Khoury, *Syria and the French Mandate: The Politics of Arab Nationalism 1920–1945*, pp. 17–18.

35. Ibid., p. 17.

36. Zenner, *A Global Community: The Jews from Aleppo, Syria*, pp. 34, 35–36.

37. Khoury, *Syria and the French Mandate: The Politics of Arab Nationalism 1920–1945*, p. 103.

38. Zenner, *A Global Community: The Jews from Aleppo, Syria,* pp. 34, 35–36.

39. Anonymous, "Treasures of the Aleppo Community," p. 12.

40. Khoury, *Syria and the French Mandate: The Politics of Arab Nationalism 1920–1945,* p. 282.

41. Ibid., p. 48.

42. Ibid., p. 11.

43. Josephus, *The War of the Jews,* Book 7, chapt. 3.

44. Ashtor, Borenstein-Makovetsky and Cohen, "Aleppo," p. 613.

45. Shamosh, *HaKeter: Sipuro shel Keter Aram Tsova,* p. 78.

46. Ibid.

47. Ibid., p. 81.

48. Zenner, *A Global Community: The Jews from Aleppo, Syria,* p. 46.

49. Ibid., pp. 41–42.

50. Ibid., p. 36.

51. Ibid., pp. 43–44.

52. Ibid., p. 45.

53, Khoury, *Syria and the French Mandate: The Politics of Arab Nationalism 1920–1945,* p. 623.

54. Anonoymous, "Treasures of the Aleppo Community," p. 11.

55. Zenner, *A Global Community: The Jews from Aleppo, Syria,* p. 81.

56. Anonymous, "Treasures of the Aleppo Community," p. 11.

57. Zenner, *A Global Community: The Jews from Aleppo, Syria,* p. 33.

58. Sutton and Kirzner, eds., *Aleppo: City of Scholars,* p. 23.

59. Alexander Dotan, *"Beit haKnesset haKadmon beHaleb veEduto shel Tik Amanuti miShnat 1710,"* p. 26; Rafael Shlomo Laniado, *Roe Yisrael,* p. 25b; and Dayan, *Holekh Tamim uPoel Tsedek,* p. 67b.

60. Zenner, *A Global Community: The Jews from Aleppo, Syria,* p. 39.

61. Alexander Dotan, *"Beit haKnesset haKadmon beHaleb veEduto shel Tik Amanuti miShnat 1710,"* p. 26; and David Cassuto, *"Beit haKnesset haAtik shel Haleb veToldotav,"* p. 86.

62. The inscription is not clear; David Cassuto, *"Beit haKnesset haAtik shel Haleb veToldotav,"* p. 86.

63. Lapidus, *Muslim Cities in the Later Middle Ages,* pp. 22, 26; and Holt et al., eds., *The Central Islamic Lands,* p. 220.

64. Zenner, *A Global Community: The Jews from Aleppo, Syria,* p. 35.

65. Alexander Dotan, *"Beit haKnesset haKadmon beHaleb veToldotav,"* p. 30.

66. Sutton and Kirzner, eds., *Aleppo: City of Scholars,* pp. 24–25.

67. Ibid.

68. Ibid., p. 26.

69. Nehmad, *"Maamar Hakira al haKeter haYakar haNikra Keter Aram Tsova,"* p. 1.

70. Adler, ed. and trans., *The Itinerary of Benjamin of Tudela,* p. 163.

71. Shamosh, *HaKeter: Sipuro shel Keter Aram Tsova,* p. 10; and Zenner, *A Global Community: The Jews from Aleppo, Syria,* p. 33.

72. Nehmad, *"Maamar Hakira al haKeter haYakar haNikra Keter Aram Tsova,"* pp. 1, 2.

73. Yitzhak Ben-Zvi; *"'Keter haTora' shel Ben-Asher,"* p. 7. This procedure was also mentioned by Faham; see Rabin, "Interview with Murad Faham," p. 2.

74. Nehmad, *"Maamar Hakira al haKeter haYakar haNikra Keter Aram Tsova,"* pp. 1–2.

75. Dayan, *Holekh Tamim uPoel Tsedek,* pp. 67b–68a.

76. Rafael Shlomo Laniado, *Sheelot uTshuvot Kise Shlomo,* p. 2:9.

77. Boyarsky, *Amude Shesh.*

78. Yitzhak Ben-Zvi; *"'Keter haTora' shel Ben-Asher,"* p. 7.

79. Ibid.

80. Zenner, *A Global Community: The Jews from Aleppo, Syria,* p. 41.

81. Khoury, *Syria and the French Mandate: The Politics of Arab Nationalism 1920–1945,* p. 143.

82. Ibid, pp. 392–393.

83. Ibid., p. 539.

84. Ibid., pp. 540–542.

85. Ibid., pp. 536–537.

86. Ibid., p. 536.

87. Ibid., p. 542–543.

88. Ibid., p. 543–544.

89. Ibid., p. 555.

90. Ibid., p. 539.

91. Ibid., p. 108.

92. Zenner, *A Global Community: The Jews from Aleppo, Syria,* pp. 80–81.

93. Ibid., p. 81.

Chapter 4

1. Shamosh, *HaKeter: Sipuro shel Keter Aram Tsova*, p. 64.

2. Ibid., p. 64.

3. Ibid., p. 65.

4. Ibid., p. 65–66.

5. Ibid.

6. Shamosh, *"Arbaim Shana veArbaim Yom beIkvot haKeter,"* pp. 108, 123. After the pogrom, however, Shamosh began to push for the recovery of the codices and even advocated their secret removal from Aleppo. His brother speculated that he changed his mind because of the tragedy that had befallen the community and the Crown, and because the community was clearly no longer capable of taking care of the codex. *Shamosh, HaKeter: Sipuro shel Keter Aram Tsova*, pp. 66, 72–73. Doubts about whether he had done the right thing, in light of what happened to the Crown in the riots, dogged Shamosh for the rest of his life. Shamosh, *"Arbaim Shana veArbaim Yom beIkvot haKeter,"* p. 108.

7. See, e.g., Shamosh, *"Arbaim Shana veArbaim Yom beIkvot haKeter,"* p. 111.

8. Ibid., pp. 123–124.

9. Shamosh, *HaKeter: Sipuro shel Keter Aram Tsova*, p. 66.

10. Ibid., p. 67. Umberto Cassuto, in *"HaTanakh shel Haleb,"* described the difficulty he had in obtaining the permission of the rabbis.

11. See Zohar, *"Shamranut Lohemet: Kavim leManhigutam haHevratit-Datit shel Hahme Haleb baEt haHadasha,"* for a discussion of incidents not related to the Crown where the rabbinic leadership of the Aleppan community displayed reactionary and anti-Zionist attitudes. For example, they opposed the establishment of a B'nai B'rith Lodge, and later, Zionist organizations; Zenner, *A Global Community: The Jews from Aleppo, Syria*, p. 46.

12. Shamosh, *HaKeter: Sipuro shel Keter Aram Tsova*, pp. 71–72.

13. Ibid., pp. 72–73.

14. Rabin, "Interview with Murad Faham," pp. 20–22.

15. Tawil, "Interview," p. 3.

16. Shamosh, *HaKeter: Sipuro shel Keter Aram Tsova*, pp. 43–44.

17. Ibid., p. 75.

18. Ibid.

19. Ofer, *"Keta miSefer Shmot mehaHelek heHaser beKeter Aram Tsova,"* p. 41.

20. Ibid., pp. 41–42.

21. Ibid., p. 42.

22. Israel Broadcasting Authority, *"HaToanim laKeter: Taalumot Keter Aram Tsova."*

23. Ibid.

24. Copy of letter with the authors.

25. Copy of letter with the authors.

26. Copy of letter with the authors.

27. Shamosh, *HaKeter: Sipuro shel Keter Aram Tsova*, pp. 72–73.

28. Ibid., p. 69.

29. Copy of the letter is with the authors. The text of the letter is reprinted at Shamosh, *HaKeter: Sipuro shel Keter Aram Tsova*, pp. 69–70.

30. Copies of letters with the authors.

31. Shamosh, *HaKeter: Sipuro shel Keter Aram Tsova*, p. 70.

32. Israel Broadcasting Authority, *"HaToanim laKeter: Taalumot Keter Aram Tsova."*

33. Ibid.

34. Shamosh, *HaKeter: Sipuro shel Keter Aram Tsova,* pp. 74–75.

35. Rabin, "Interview with Murad Faham," p. 1.

36. Ibid., pp. 1, 2–4.

37. Ibid., pp. 1–2.

38. Ibid., p. 9.

39. Ibid., pp. 10–12.

40. Ibid., pp. 12–16.

41. Ibid., pp. 22–25.

42. Ibid., pp. 22–25

43. Ibid., pp. 25–38.

44. Ibid., pp. 25–39.

45. Ibid., p. 40.

46. Ibid., pp. 40–41.

47. It is unclear whether this story has any basis in fact, particularly as it seems unlikely that the Syrian government would have agreed under any circumstances to return the codex to the Jewish community if it had indeed obtained possession of it. The story may have been an attempt by the Allepan rabbis to transfer responsibility for the damage to the Crown, or for its departure from Aleppo, to the Syrian government.

48. Ibid., pp. 42–43.

49. Ibid., p. 43.

50. Ibid., p. 44

51. Israel Broadcasting Authority, *"HaToanim laKeter: Taalumot Keter Aram Tsova."*

Chapter 5

1. Copy of letter with the authors.

2. Copy of letter with the authors.

3. Rabin, "Interview with Murad Faham," p. 44.

4. Ibid., pp. 44–46.

5. Ibid., p. 46.

6. *Shtar Hekdesh.*

7. Ibid.

8. Shamosh, *HaKeter: Sipuro shel Keter Aram Tsova*, p. 111.

9. Ibid., p. 112.

10. Ibid., p. 112.

11. Ibid., p. 110.

12. Available at www.aleppocodex.org.

13. Shamosh, *HaKeter: Sipuro shel Keter Aram Tsova*, pp. 109–110.

14. Ibid., p. 110.

15. Ibid., p. 110.

16. Ofer, "The History and Authority of the Aleppo Codex," p. 44; and *"Daat Torah,"* copy with the authors.

17. Shamosh, *HaKeter: Sipuro shel Keter Aram Tsova*, p. 122.

18. Ibid., p. 122.

19. Ibid., p. 104.

20. Ibid., p. 122.

21. Beit-Arié, *"Daf Nosaf le Keter Aram Tsova."*

22. Four songs are written in one column, with the text immediately preceding and following the songs written in one column or two uneven columns. The songs are: the Song of Moses (*Haazinu*), Deuteronomy 32:1–52; the song of Deborah, Judges 5; the Song of David, 2 Samuel 22; and David's Song for Asaph, 1 Chronicles 16:8–36. Presumably the Song of the Sea (*Az Yashir*), Exodus 15:1–18, now lost, was written similarly. It is not clear whether these unique column formats were meant to indicate how the verses surrounding the songs should be written in a Torah Scroll."

23. Yitzhak Ben-Zvi, "'*Keter haTora' shel Ben-Asher*," p. 1.

24. Shamosh, "*Arbaim Shana veArbaim Yom beIkvot haKeter,*" p. 110; and Beit-Arié, "*Daf Nosaf leKeter Aram Tsova.*"

25. Yitzhak Ben-Zvi. "'*Keter haTora' shel Ben-Asher*," p. 1.

26. Shamosh, *HaKeter: Sipuro shel Keter Aram Tsova*, p. 122.

27. Ibid., pp. 171–174.

28. Ibid., p. 122.

29. Ibid., p. 116.

30. Ibid., pp. 116–117.

31. Israel Broadcasting Authority, *HaToanim laKeter: Taalumot Keter Aram Tsova.*

32. Ibid.

33. Ibid.

34. Polachek, "Fungi Not Fire Damaged Aleppo Codex," p. 203.

35. Maggen, "Conservation of the Aleppo Codex," pp. 123–127.

36. Letters from Murad Faham, copies with the authors.

37. Copy with the authors.

38. Copy with the authors.

39. These follow the order in the Babylonian Talmud *Baba Batra* 14b.

40. Shamosh, *HaKeter: Sipuro shel Keter Aram Tsova*, pp. 120–121.

41. Ibid., p. 122.

42. Beit-Arié, *"Daf Nosaf le Keter Aram Tsova."*

43. Yitzhak Ben-Zvi, *"'Keter ha Tora' shel Ben-Asher,"* pp. 1–2.

44. Wickes, *A Treatise on the Accentuation of the Twenty-One So-Called Prose Books of the Old Testament*. The page was republished in *Textus*, Vol. 1.

45. Shamosh, *HaKeter: Sipuro shel Keter Aram Tsova*, pp. 50, 52.

46. Ibid.

47. Ibid., pp. 60–63.

48. See Segall, *Travels through Northern Syria*, p. 99; and Goshen-Gottstein, "A Recovered Part of the Aleppo Codex."

49. Shamosh, *HaKeter: Sipuro shel Keter Aram Tsova*, pp. 31, 54.

50. Pfeffer, "Fragment of Ancient Parchment from Bible Given to Jerusalem Scholars."

51. Yitzhak Ben-Zvi, *"'Keter ha Tora' shel Ben-Asher,"* pp. 7–8.

52. Shamosh, *HaKeter: Sipuro shel Keter Aram Tsova*, p. 57.

53. Ibid., pp. 57–58.

54. Penkower, *Nusah ha Tora be Keter Aram Tsova — Edut Hadasha*, pp. 10–11.

55. Shamosh, *HaKeter: Sipuro shel Keter Aram Tsova*, p. 25.

56. Ofer, "The History and Authority of the Aleppo Codex," pp. 40–41.

57. Ibid., p. 40.

58. Ibid., pp. 41–42.

Chapter 6

1. The curses begin at Deuteronomy 28:15; the first extant page of the Crown begins with the last word of 28:16.

2. A recent book on the Aleppan community in Flatbush, New York, includes a detailed if highly unscholarly section on the Crown; Sutton and Kirzner, eds., *Aleppo: City of Scholars.* For a critical analysis of this volume, see Zohar, "And Art Scroll Created Aleppo in Its Own Image."

3. Israel Broadcasting Authority, *HaToanim laKeter: Taalumot Keter Aram Tsova.*

4. Conversation between Dr. Hayim Tawil and Shlomo Gal, Tel Aviv, 1992; notes with the authors.

Aleppo

Aleppo is a city in northern Syria, near the border with Turkey. It is one of the oldest continuously inhabited cities in the world and was initially built on a small group of hills surrounding the prominent rise where the Citadel of Aleppo currently stands. Historically, the city's importance was due to its strategic location midway between the Mediterranean Sea and the Euphrates River, at the crossroads of two major trade routes. This allowed the city to mediate the trade between Iraq, Persia, and India to the east and Syria, Lebanon, and southern Turkey. Beginning in the early 20th century, other trading centers superseded Aleppo, and the city's economic importance has declined steadily since. It had a Jewish community from at least the 5th century c.e. until the 20th century.

Aleppo pogrom

After the United Nations vote on November 29, 1947, in favor of the partition of the Land of Israel, the Arabs inhabitants of Aleppo rioted. A number of Jews were killed, and many were injured; the community went into terminal decline soon thereafter. During the pogrom, the Crown of Aleppo was damaged and subsequently lost. Part of the Crown reappeared in Israel in 1958.

Ben Asher, Aharon ben Moshe

Aharon ben Moshe ben Asher (10th century C.E.) lived and worked in the city of Tiberias on the western shore of the Sea of Galilee. He was descended from a long line of Masoretes; his father, Moshe ben Asher, is credited with writing the Cairo Codex of the Prophets (ca. 895). Aharon ben Asher refined the Tiberian system for noting vowel sounds in Hebrew that is still in use today. Perhaps most important, Aharon Ben Asher worked with Shlomo Ben Buya'a to create the Crown of Aleppo, also known as the Aleppo Codex; he added the vowelization, cantillation signs, and Masoretic notes to the codex. For more than a thousand years, he has been regarded by Jews around the world as having produced the most authoritative version of the Masoretic text.

Ben-Zvi Institute

The Ben-Zvi Institute *(Yad Yitzhak Ben-Zvi)* is a non-profit organization chartered by a special law of the Knesset, the Israeli parliament. The institute focuses on the scholarly interests of Yitzhak Ben-Zvi, Israel's second president. It is a leader in research and education in the areas of the history and culture of the Land of Israel, Jerusalem studies, and the study of the *Mizrahi* Jewish communities. The institute holds the Crown of Aleppo in trust for the Jewish people. It is located in Jerusalem's historic Rehavia neighborhood and is housed in the former presidential quarters where president Yitzhak Ben-Zvi and his successor, Zalman Shazar, resided and carried out their official duties.

Ben-Zvi, Yitzhak

Yitzhak Ben-Zvi (November 24, 1884 – April 23, 1963) was a historian, a Labor Zionist leader, and the second and longest-serving president of Israel. Born in Poltava, Ukraine, Ben-Zvi was the eldest son of Zvi Shimshelevitz, from whose first name he derived his Hebraicized surname. He became an active Zionist after the 1905 Kishinev pogroms and was a representative to the Zionist Congress of 1907; he emigrated to Israel that same year. Ben-Zvi helped found the *Ahdut haAvoda* Party and was active in the Haganah, the Jewish defense force, formed in response to the Arab Riots of 1920, which became the core of the Israel Defense Forces. Ben-Zvi was among the signers of Israel's Declaration of Independence on Friday, May 14, 1948, and he served in the First and Second Knesset for the *Mapai* Party. He was elected president of Israel on December 8, 1952, a position he retained until his death in 1963. Beyond his governmental duties, Ben-Zvi was active in scholarly research, particularly in the study of *Mizrahi* Jewish communities, and he worked tirelessly to repatriate the Crown of Aleppo.

Bible See TANAKH.

Cantillation

Cantillation is the ritual chanting of readings from the Bible in synagogue services. The chants are rendered in accordance with the special signs or marks printed in the Masoretic text of the Bible to complement the letters and vowel points. These marks are known as *taame hamikra* or simply *taamim* in Hebrew. The notation system was perfected in Tiberias in the 10th century c.e., and its premier example is found in the Crown of Aleppo.

A primary purpose of the cantillation signs is to guide the reading of the Bible in the synagogue. Generally, each word of text has a cantillation mark at its primary accent, and associated with that mark is a musical phrase that tells the reader how to sing the word. There are two systems of cantillation signs in the Bible: one is used in the 21 prose books; the other appears in the three poetical books of Psalms, Proverbs, and Job. The music associated with the signs varies among Jewish communities.

Less well known is the fact that the cantillation signs also provide information on the syntactical structure of the text. According to some scholars, they are a commentary on the text itself, highlighting important ideas musically. The tropes are not random strings but follow a set and describable grammar. The very word *taam,* which means "taste" or "sense," indicates that the pauses and intonation denoted by the accents (with or without formal musical rendition) bring out the sense of the passage.

Thus the cantillation signs serve three functions. First, they have musical value, and reading the Bible with cantillation becomes a musical chant, in which the music itself serves as a way of conveying the proper accentuation and syntax. Second, they divide the verses into smaller units of meaning, a function that gives them a limited but sometimes important role in exegesis. This function is accomplished through the use of various disjunctive and conjunctive signs that together indicate how the words should be connected in phrases. (The disjunctive signs can be roughly compared to modern punctuation marks.) Finally, most of the signs indicate the specific syllable of stress in the word.

Cassuto, Umberto

Umberto Cassuto, also known as Moshe David Cassuto (1883–1951), was a rabbi and biblical scholar born in Florence, Italy. He studied at the University of Florence and the Collegio Rabbinico. After receiving a degree and rabbinical ordination, he taught at both institutions. From 1914 to 1925, he was chief rabbi of Florence. In 1925 he became professor of Hebrew language and literature at the University of Florence and then assumed the Hebrew language chair at the University of Rome La Sapienza. When the Fascists passed anti-Semitic laws in 1938 that barred Jews from teaching or studying at Italian universities, Cassuto accepted an invitation to join the faculty of the Hebrew University of Jerusalem.

Cassuto's *Documentary Hypothesis and the Composition of the Pentateuch* was one of the first mainstream works to offer a detailed critique of the "documentary hypothesis," which argued that the Torah had its origins in separate documents that were combined by editors into the text with which we are familiar today. Cassuto saw the need to produce the most accurate possible text of the Bible. He realized that most biblical texts that had been published until his time had been edited by non-Jews or apostates to Christianity, and that Christian biases had thus crept into the text, particularly in the form of the chapter divisions. Cassuto sought out the oldest and most reliable manuscripts of the Bible, dating back many centuries before the invention of printing. In particular, in 1943 he managed to visit the Great Synagogue of Aleppo and study the Crown of Aleppo. He was the last known outside scholar to study this most important Jewish manuscript before it was damaged in the pogrom of 1947. Cassuto's edition of the Bible was published posthumously in 1953. He also wrote a Hebrew commentary on the Bible that is widely known in Israel.

Codex

A codex is a manuscript produced in the format used for modern books, with separate pages bound together between covers. The codex was invented by the

Romans and gradually replaced the scroll. Although technically any modern printed book is a codex, the term is used specifically for manuscript books produced from late antiquity through the Middle Ages.

Colophon

The term colophon, from the Greek word for "summit" or "finishing touch," refers to the inscription at the end of a manuscript. The colophon usually contains information regarding the persons associated with the text, the occasion for or the purpose of writing the manuscript, or a discussion of the text. In terms of its position, the colophon is comparable to a signature line today. Bibliographically, however, it more closely resembles the imprint page in a modern book.

Faham, Murad (Mordechai)

Murad (Mordechai) Faham was born in Aleppo in 1904 and inherited a cheese-making business from his father. He subsequently became involved in helping the Jewish community of Aleppo, which led to his imprisonment and expulsion from Syria. During a brief return visit to Aleppo to settle his affairs, he was asked to take the Crown of Aleppo to safety in Israel. At great personal risk, he agreed and delivered the Crown to President Yitzhak Ben-Zvi.

Firkovich, Abraham

Abraham Firkovich was born in a small village outside Luck, Poland, in 1786. After studying the principles of the Karaite religion, he settled in Crimea. Motivated initially by a desire to prove the superiority of the Karaites over the Rabbanites, Firkovich amassed a large collection of Hebrew manuscripts, which was subsequently acquired by the Imperial Library in St. Petersburg, now the Russian National Library. Among these manuscripts is the famous Leningrad Codex. Firkovich also attempted to acquire the Crown of Aleppo but was rebuffed.

Fostat

Fostat was the first capital of Egypt under Arab rule. It was built by the Arab general 'Amr ibn al-'As immediately after the Arab conquest of Egypt in 641

C.E. and featured the Mosque of Amr, the first mosque ever built in Egypt. The city reached its peak in the 12th century, when it had a population of approximately 200,000. It was the center of administrative power in Egypt until it was ordered burned in 1168 by the vizier Shawar to keep its wealth out of the hands of the invading Crusaders. The remains of the city were eventually absorbed into nearby Cairo (which had been established to the north of Fostat in 969, when the Tunisian Fatimids conquered the region and created the city as a royal enclosure for the caliph). Subsequently, the area of Fostat fell into disrepair for hundreds of years and was used as a garbage dump. Today, Fostat is part of Old Cairo, with few buildings remaining from its days as the capital. Archaeological digs, however, have uncovered a wealth of material in the area.

Great Synagogue of Aleppo

The Great Synagogue of Aleppo has been a Jewish place of worship since at least the 8th century C.E. It is also known as the Yellow (*Al-Safra*) Synagogue, the Ancient Synagogue, and the Synagogue of Yoav ben Tseruya. The synagogue was the home of the Crown of Aleppo for almost 500 years, until the Aleppo Pogrom of 1947. The synagogue still stands but is inactive, now that the last of Aleppo's Jews have escaped Syria.

Jerusalem

Jerusalem is the capital of Israel and its largest city in both population and area, with approximately 750,000 residents living in the 48.3 square miles (125.1 square kilometers) that make up Greater Jerusalem. The city is located in the Judean Mountains, between the Mediterranean Sea and the northern tip of the Dead Sea, and today consists of the Old City and the New City. The Old City, which encompasses only 0.35 square miles (0.91 square kilometers), has a history that goes back to the 4th millennium B.C.E., making it one of the oldest cities in the world. Jerusalem has been the holiest city in Judaism and the spiritual center of the Jewish people since the 10th century B.C.E. It also contains sites holy to Christianity and Islam. In the course of its history, Jerusalem has been destroyed twice, besieged more than 20 times, and repeatedly attacked. Control of Jerusalem has changed hands many times over the last three millennia.

Karaites

Karaites are members of a Jewish sect that recognizes only the Bible as holy writ and rejects Rabbinic Judaism and the Oral Law (that is, the Mishnah and the Talmud and the legal system based on them). The movement crystallized in Baghdad, in present-day Iraq. In interpreting the Bible, Karaites strive to adhere to the plain meaning of the text.

Ktiv haser

Ktiv haser, literally "defective writing," is Hebrew writing whose consonants match those generally used in voweled text, but without the vowelization. Without these marks, the text is difficult to read, and the reader must make use of the context to be sure of the correct reading. A typical example of a Hebrew text written in *ktiv haser* is the Torah scroll used in the synagogue.

Ktiv male

Ktiv male, literally "full writing," is a modified Hebrew spelling often used because of the difficulties posed by unvoweled Hebrew text. This system mostly involves the addition of the letters *"vav"* and *"yud"* to mark the different vowels. It has become widely used wherever the vowel signs are not included; most modern Hebrew texts are published in *ktiv male*.

Leningrad Codex

The Leningrad Codex is one of the oldest manuscripts of the complete Hebrew Bible produced according to the Tiberian Masorah; it is dated to 1008 according to its colophon. The Crown of Aleppo, against which the Leningrad Codex was corrected, was the first such manuscript, dating to the 10th century, but parts of it have been missing since 1947; thus the Leningrad Codex is the oldest complete codex of the Tiberian Masorah that has survived intact. The Leningrad Codex is so named because it has been housed at the Russian National Library, then known as the Imperial Library, in St. Petersburg since it was acquired by the library from Abraham Firkovich in 1863 and accessioned as Firkovich B 19 A. Firkovich gave no indication in his writings as to where he acquired it. Originally, the codex was known as Codex Petersburgensis or Petropolensis, or the St. Petersburg Codex. After the Russian Revolution, scholars renamed it the Leningrad Codex, and at the request of the library this name continues to be used, despite the fact that the city is once again known as St. Petersburg.

Maimonides

Maimonides was born around 1135 in Córdoba, Spain. Also known as the Rambam — the Hebrew acronym of his full name and title, Rabbi Moshe ben Maimon — he is widely regarded as one of the greatest scholars in Jewish history. Following a sojourn in Morocco, Maimonides lived briefly in Israel before settling in Fostat, Egypt, where he served as physician to Grand Vizier Al-Fadhil and Sultan Saladin of Egypt, and where he composed most of his works, including the *Mishneh Torah*. He died in Fostat in 1204 and was subsequently buried in Tiberias.

Masoretes

The Masoretes were scribes and Bible scholars working between the 7th and 11th centuries. They were based primarily in Israel, in the cities of Tiberias and Jerusalem, as well as in Babylonia. Each of these three groups compiled a system of pronunciation and grammatical guides in the form of diacritical notes on the text of the Bible, in an attempt to fix its pronunciation, paragraph and verse divisions, and cantillation. The two schools of the Ben Ashers and the Ben Naftalis together devised the Tiberian vowel and cantillation notation systems that are still in use today.

Matres lectionis

Matres lectionis, Latin for "mothers of reading," are consonants used in the spelling of some Semitic languages to indicate vowels. They are found in Ugaritic, Moabite, and Phoenician but are widely used only in Hebrew, Aramaic, Syriac, and Arabic. In Hebrew, they are known as *imot hakriya;* the letters *"aleph," "he," "vav,"* and *"yud"* are used in this fashion. In the absence of these letters, unambiguous reading of an unvocalized text is difficult. For example, in the word "bet" ("the house of," spelled *"bet-yud-tav"*), the *"yud"* indicates a vowel. Without the "yud," the letters *"bet"* and *"tav"* would be taken to spell the word *"bat"* or "daughter." (By contrast, in the word "bayit" or "house," which is spelled with the same letters, the "yud" functions as a genuine consonant.) When words can be written either with or without *matres lectionis,* spellings that include these letters are called *ktiv male* or "full" (plene); spellings without them are called *ktiv haser* or "defective." In the 9th century, it was decided that the system of *matres lectionis* was insufficient for indicating the vowels precisely enough, so a supplemental vowelization system consisting of diacritical symbols or *nekudot* joined *matres lectionis* as part of the Hebrew writing system.

Mizrahi Jews

Mizrahi Jews, literally "Eastern" Jews, are descended from the Jewish communities of the Middle East, North Africa, Central Asia, and the Caucasus. With the exception of Yemenite and Ethiopian Jews, who are sometimes included but are more often considered to make up groups in their own right, *Mizrahi* Jews are those originating from the Arab world and adjacent countries. Despite their heterogeneous origins, most *Mizrahi* Jews observe customs similar to those of Spanish *(Sefardi)* Jews, due to the dispersion of Spanish Jews throughout the Muslim world. This has led to the conflation of the terms *Sefardi* and *Mizrahi* in colloquial Hebrew usage.

Musta'arabim

Musta'arabim or "Arabized" Jews are Arabic-speaking Jews who lived in the Middle East before the expulsion of the Jews from Spain in 1492. After the expulsion, Spanish-Jewish exiles moved to the Middle East and settled among their Arabic-speaking, or Hebreo-Arabic-speaking, co-religionists. In many countries, these Spanish-Jewish immigrants and the older, established Jewish communities maintained separate synagogues and separate religious rituals but often had a common rabbinate. Over time, the communities and their customs tended to merge. Among Syrian Jews, the *Musta'arabim* have assimilated with the Spanish Jews and are no longer a distinct entity, although certain families continue to identify themselves as Spanish Jews.

Rabbanism

Rabbanism is the primary religious stream of Judaism. It evolved after the destruction of the Second Temple by the Roman Empire in 70 C.E., when it became impossible to practice the religious customs and ritual animal sacrifices that were at that time central to Jewish observance. Rabbinic Judaism developed as a successor system between the 2nd and 6th centuries, with the development of the Mishnah and Talmud as guides to the interpretation of the Bible. Mainstream Rabbinic Judaism differs most sharply from Karaite Judaism, which disputes the validity of the Oral Law and the Rabbanite approach to interpreting the Bible. Although there are today profound differences among the major Jewish denominations with respect to the binding force of Jewish law and the willingness to challenge precedent, all identify themselves as coming from the Rabbinic tradition.

Sefardi

The term *"Sefardi,"* also spelled *"Sephardi,"* refers, strictly speaking, to Jews originally from the Iberian Peninsula (modern Spain and Portugal) and their practices. Included in this designation are the descendants of Jews expelled from Spain under the Alhambra Decree of 1492 or from Portugal by order of King Manuel I in 1497, as well as the descendants of crypto-Jews who left the peninsula in later centuries. The name comes from *Sfarad,* a Biblical location that was subsequently identified with the Iberian Peninsula; the word *"Sfarad"* means "Spain" in modern Hebrew. For religious purposes, and in modern Israel, *Sefardi* is sometimes used loosely to include most Jews of Asian and African origin who now follow, to a greater or lesser extent, the Spanish liturgy and customs. The liturgy and customs of most Eastern European Jews, including Hasidim, are also loosely referred to as *Sefardi* because they are partially based on the traditions of Rabbi Isaac Luria of Safed, the prominent 16th-century *Mizrahi* mystic.

Tanakh

Tanakh is a Hebrew acronym formed from the initial Hebrew letters of the Bible's three traditional subdivisions: the Torah (the Five Books of Moses), Neviim (Prophets), and Ketuvim (Writings). It is the most common term used for the Bible in modern Hebrew. In English, the Tanakh is often referred to as the Hebrew or Jewish Bible, to distinguish it clearly from the Christian Bible. The books of the Tanakh are incorporated in various forms in Christian Bibles, where they are referred to as the "Old Testament." The term "Old

Testament" is not generally used by Jews, as it reflects the Christian notion that the Christian Bible has superseded the TANAKH.

The chapter divisions and verse numbers commonly used in printed editions of the TANAKH have no basis in the Jewish tradition. Originating with the anti-Jewish medieval clerical debates in Spain, they reflect instead Christian exegesis of the Bible and ignore the accepted closed and open sections of the Masorah. Similarly, the division of Samuel, Kings, and Chronicles into two books each contradicts the original text.

Because of their longstanding and widespread use, these book chapters and verse divisions continue to be used, but in more recent years their impact and prominence on the printed page have been reduced. Many editions have accomplished this by removing the divisions from the text itself and relegating them to the margins of the page, thereby restoring the standing of the weekly portions and the open and closed sections. One publisher, Koren, has even introduced a new chapter system that is more faithful to the Masorah.

Tiberias

Tiberias is a town on the western shore of the Sea of Galilee in Israel. It was built in about 20 C.E. by Herod Antipas, the son of Herod the Great, on the site of the destroyed village of Rakat, and it became the capital of his realm in Galilee. It was named in honor of the Roman emperor Tiberius. At one time, Tiberias was the center of Jewish culture. The Sanhedrin moved there, and the Jerusalem Talmud was largely composed there. Under Byzantine and Arab rule, however, Tiberias declined and was devastated by wars and earthquakes. Even so, a community of Masoretes flourished in the town from the beginning of the 8th century to the end of the 10th century. These scholars created a comprehensive system for representing Hebrew vocalization, which became the accepted notational standard. Aharon ben Asher, who refined the vocalization method now know as the Tiberian system and added the vocalization and cantillation signs to the Crown of Aleppo, is considered the greatest Tiberian Masoretic scholar.

Abrahams, Israel and Cecil Roth. "Cassuto, Umberto." In *Encyclopaedia Judaica*, 2nd edition, edited by Michael Berenbaum and Fred Skolnik, 4:510–511. Detroit: Macmillan Reference USA, 2007.

Abramsky, Samuel, Shimon Gibson, Michael Avi-Yonah, Menahem Stern, Eliyahu Ashtor and Haïm Z'ew Hirschberg. "Jerusalem." In *Encyclopaedia Judaica*, 2nd edition, edited by Michael Berenbaum and Fred Skolnik, 11:143–232. Detroit: Macmillan Reference USA, 2007.

Adler, Elhanan Nathan. "Aleppo." In *Gedenkbuch zur Erinnerung an David Kaufmann* (Memorial Book for David Kaufmann), edited by M. Brann and F. Rosenthal, 128–143. Breslau: Schottlaender, 1900.

Adler, Marcus Nathan, ed. and trans. *The Itinerary of Benjamin of Tudela*. London: Oxford University Press, 1907.

Allony, Nehemya. *"HaSefer uMelekhet haSefer beErets Yisrael Bime haBenayim"* ("The Book and Bookmaking in the Land of Israel in the Middle Ages"). *Shalem* 4 (1984): 1–25.

———. *"Heeteke Keter Aram Tsova beYerushalayim uvaGola"* ("Copies of the Crown of Aleppo in Jerusalem and the Exile"). *Beit Mikra* 24 (1979): 193–204.

———. *"Iyunim beKetav haHakdasha shel Keter Aram Tsova"* ("Investigations in the Dedication of the Crown of Aleppo"). *Be'er Sheva* 2 (1984): 27–56.

————. *"Rambam, Ben Asher uBen Bouya Meshamshim Keter Aram Tsova"* ("Maimonides, Ben Asher, Ben Buya'a and the Crown of Aleppo"). *Tarbiz* 50 (1981): 348–370.

————. *"Sefer haTora vehaMitshaf beKriyat haTora beTsibur beAdat haRabanim uveAdat haKaraim"* ("Scroll and Codex in Public Reading of the Torah among the Rabbanites and Karaites"). *Beit Mikra* 76 (1979): 321–134.

————. *"Tveria beYeme haBenayim"* ("Tiberias in the Middle Ages"). In *HaBalshanut haIvrit beTveria (The Tiberian School of Hebrew Grammar)*, 9–31. Jerusalem: Mass, 1995.

Anonymous. *Keter Yerushalayim (The Jerusalem Crown)*. Jerusalem: Hebrew University Press, 2002.

Anonymous. *Treasures of the Aleppo Community*. Jerusalem: Israel Museum, 1988.

Ashtor, Eliyahu A. *A History of the Jews in Egypt and Syria*. 3 vols. Jerusalem: Kook, 1944–1970.

Ashtor, Eliyahu, Leah Borenstein-Makovetsky, Hayyim J. Cohen and Amnon Shiloah. "Aleppo." In *Encyclopaedia Judaica*, 2nd edition, edited by Michael Berenbaum and Fred Skolnik, 1:613–617. Detroit: Macmillan Reference USA, 2007.

Ashtor, Eliyahu, Avraham Yaari, and Haim J. Cohen. "Cairo." In *Encyclopaedia Judaica*, 2nd edition, edited by Michael Berenbaum and Fred Skolnik, 4:342–346. Detroit: Macmillan Reference USA, 2007.

Assaf, Simha, and L. A. Mayer. "Tiberias." In *sefer HaYishuv (The Book of the Yishuv)*. Vol. 2: *Mime Kibush Erets Yisrael al yede haAravim vead Masaei haTslav (From the Arab Conquest of the Land of Israel to the Crusades)*, edited by Simha Assaf and L. A. Mayer, 9–14. Jerusalem: Bialik, 1944.

Avi-Yonah, Michael, Abraham J. Brawer, Efraim Orni and Shimon Gibson. "Tiberias." In *Encyclopaedia Judaica*, 2nd edition, edited by Michael Berenbaum and Fred Skolnik, 19:714–716. Detroit: Macmillan Reference USA, 2007.

Beit-Arié, Malachi. *"Daf Nosaf leKeter Aram Tsova"* ("A Lost Leaf from the Aleppo Codex Recovered"). *Tarbiz* 51 (1982): 171–174.

Ben-Hayyim, Zeev. "Ben Asher, Aaron ben Moses." In *Encyclopaedia Judaica*, 2nd edition, edited by Michael Berenbaum and Fred Skolnik, 3:319–321. Detroit: Macmillan Reference USA, 2007.

Ben-Sasson, Menahem. "The Bible and the Hebrew University of Jerusalem." In *The Jerusalem Crown Companion Volume*, edited by Mordechai Glatzer, 3–8.

Jerusalem: Hebrew University Press, 2002.

Ben-Shammai, Haggai. "Firkovich, Abraham." In *Encyclopaedia Judaica*, 2nd edition, edited by Michael Berenbaum and Fred Skolnik, 7:44–45. Detroit: Macmillan Reference USA, 2007.

———"*Hearot leGilgulav shel Keter Aram Tsova*" ("Notes on the Peregrinations of the Codex of Aleppo"). In *Erets uMeloa: Mehkarim beToldot Kehilat Aram Tsova (Haleb) veTarbuta (Aleppo Studies, The Jews of Aleppo: Their History and Culture)*, edited by Yaron Harel, Yom Tov Asis and Miriam Frenkel. Jerusalem: Ben-Zvi Institute, 2009.

Ben-Zvi, Rahel Yanait. *BiShlihut laLevanon uleSuriya, 1943 (Mission to Lebanon and Syria, 1943)*. Tel Aviv: Malo, 1979.

Ben-Zvi, Yitzhak. "*'Keter haTora' shel Ben-Asher*" ("The 'Bible Crown' of Ben Asher"). In *Kitve Mifal haMikra shel haUniversita haIvrit (The Hebrew University Bible Project Series)*. Vol. 1: *Mehkarim beKeter Aram Tsova (Studies in the Crown of Aleppo)*, edited by Chaim Rabin, 1–9. Jerusalem: Hebrew University Press, 1968.

———. "The Codex of Ben-Asher." *Textus* 1 (1960): 1–16.

———. "*'Keter haTora' shel Ben-Asher Shenikhtav beErets Yisrael*" ("The Codex of Ben-Asher That Was Written in the Land of Israel"). *Sinai* 43 (1957–1958): 5–13.

———. "*'Keter haTora' shel Ben-Asher Shenikhtav beErets Yisrael Ud Mutsal meEsh*" ("The Bible Crown of Ben-Asher Written in the Land of Israel: A Firebrand Saved from the Fire"). In *Ale Asor*, edited by Judah Leib Maimon. Jerusalem: Kook, 1958.

Benisch, A., ed. *The Travels of Rabbi Petachia of Ratisbon*. London: Trubner & Co., 1856.

Bostom, Andrew G., ed. *The Legacy of Jihad: Islamic Holy War and the Fate of Non-Muslims*. Amherst, N.Y.: Prometheus Books, 2005.

Bosworth, C. E., E. van Donzel, W. P. Henreich, and G. Lecomte, eds. *The Encyclopaedia of Islam*, vol. 9. Leiden: Brill, 1996.

Boyarsky, Shmuel Shlomo. *Amude Shesh*. Jerusalem: Shaar Keter Torah, 1892.

Breuer, Mordechai. *Keter Aram Tsova vehaNusah haMekubal shel haMikra (The Aleppo Codex and the Accepted Text of the Bible)*. Jerusalem: Kook, 1976.

———. *Torah, Neviim, Ketuvim Mughim al pi haNusah vehaMesora shel Keter Aram Tsova veKitve haYad haKrovim Lo (The Pentateuch, Prophets, and Writings According to the Text and Masorah of the Aleppo Codex and Related Manuscripts)*. 3 vols. Jerusalem: Kook, 1977–1982 (Republished in 2 vols., 1997; in 1 vol., 1989).

Browne, Mallory. "Jews in Grave Danger in All Moslem Lands." *New York Times,* May 16, 1948, p. E4.

Cassuto, David. *"Beit haKneset haAtik shel Haleb veToldotav"* ("The Ancient Synagogue of Aleppo and Its History"). *Pe'amim* (1998): 84–105.

Cassuto, Umberto [Moshe David]. *"HaTanakh shel Haleb"* ("The Aleppo Bible"). *Haaretz,* Jan. 2, 1948.

Dayan, Abraham. *Holekh Tamim uPoel Tsedek (Innocent and Righteous).* Leghorn: Ottolenghi, 1849.

Dotan, Aron. "Ben Asher, Moses." In *Encyclopaedia Judaica,* 2nd edition, edited by Michael Berenbaum and Fred Skolnik, 3:321. Detroit: Macmillan Reference USA, 2007.

———. *Ben Asher's Creed: A Study of the History of the Controversy.* Masoretic Studies Series No. 3, edited by Harry M. Orlinsky. Missoula, Mont.: Scholars Press, 1977.

———. *"HaOmnam Haya Ben Asher Karai?"* ("Was Ben Asher Indeed a Karaite?"). In *The Canon and Masorah of the Hebrew Bible: An Introductory Reader,* edited by S. Z. Leiman, 716–745. New York: Ktav, 1974.

———. "Masorah." In *Encyclopaedia Judaica,* 2nd edition, edited by Michael Berenbaum and Fred Skolnik, 13:603–656. Detroit: Macmillan Reference USA, 2007.

———, ed. *Biblia Hebraica Leningradensia: Prepared According to the Vocalization, Accents, and Masora of Aaron ben Moses ben Asher in the Leningrad Codex.* Reprint. Peabody, Mass.: Hendrickson, 2001.

Dotan (Lutzki), Alexander. *"Beit haKneset haKadmon beHaleb veEduto shel Tik Amanuti miShnat 1710"* ("The History of the Ancient Synagogue of Aleppo and the Testimony of a Decorative Case from 1710"). *Sefunot* 1 (1957): 25–61.

Dudman, Helga. *Tiberias.* Jerusalem: Carta, 1988.

Elkin, Ze'ev, and Menahem Ben-Sasson. *"Avraham Firkovich uGenizat Kahir"* ("Abraham Firkovitch and the Cairo Geniza"). *Pe'amim* 90 (2002): 51–95.

Elliger, K., and Willhelm Rudolph. *Biblia Hebraica Stuttgartensia.* Stuttgart: Deutsche Bibelgeselleschaft, 1977.

Gil, Moshe. *A History of Palestine, 634–1099,* translated by Ethel Broido. Cambridge: Cambridge University Press, 1997.

Glatzer, Mordechai, "The Book of Books—From Scroll to Codex and into Print." In *The Jerusalem Crown Companion Volume*, edited by Mordechai Glatzer, 61–101. Jerusalem: Hebrew University Press, 2002.

———. *"Melekhet haSefer beKeter Aram Tsova veHashlakhoteha"* ("The Aleppo Codex: Codicological and Paleographical Aspects"). *Sefunot* 19 (1989): 167–276.

Goitein, S. D. *HaYishuv beErets Yisrael beReshit haIslam ubeTekufat haTsalbanim leOr Kitve haGeniza (Jewry in the Land of Israel in Early Islamic and Crusader Times in Light of the Genizah Documents)*. Jerusalem: Ben-Zvi Institute, 1980.

Goshen-Gottstein, Moshe H. "The Aleppo Codex and the Rise of the Masoretic Bible Text." *Biblical Archaeologist* 42 (Summer 1979): 145–162.

———. "The Authenticity of the Aleppo Codex." *Textus* 1 (1960): 17–58.

———. "Biblical Manuscripts in the United States." *Textus* 2 (1962): 28–59.

———. *"HaOtentiut shel Keter Haleb"* ("The Authenticity of the Crown of Aleppo"). In *Kitve Mifal haMikra shel haUniversita haIvrit (The Hebrew University Bible Project Series)*. Vol. 1: *Mehkarim beKeter Aram Tsova (Studies in the Crown of Aleppo)*, edited by Chaim Rabin, 10–37. Jerusalem: Hebrew University Press, 1960.

———. "A Recovered Part of the Aleppo Codex." *Textus* 5 (1966): 53–59.

———. "The Rise of the Tiberian Bible Text." In *Biblical and Other Studies*, edited by Alexander Altman, 79–122. Cambridge: Harvard University Press, 1963.

Grätz, Heinrich. *"Die beiden Ben-Ascher und die Masora"* ("Ben-Asher and the Masorah"). *Monatsschrift für Geschichte und Wissenschaft des Judentums* 20 (1871): 1–12, 49–59.

Harkavy, Abraham. A. *Altjudische Denkmaler aus der Krim (Ancient Jewish Monuments from the Crimea)*. St. Petersburg: M. Eggers, 1876.

Harkavy, Abraham, and Hermann Leberecht Strack. *Catalog der hebräischen Bibelhandschriften der Kaiserlichen-öffentlichen Bibliothek in St. Petersburg (Catalogue of the Hebrew Bible Manuscripts in the Imperial Public Library in St. Petersburg)*. St. Petersburg: Ricker, 1875.

Haron, Miriam Joyce. *Palestine and the Anglo-American Connection, 1945–1950*. New York: Lang, 1986.

Hitti, Philip K. *History of Syria*. London: Macmillan, 1951.

Hofman, Shlomo. "Karaites." In *Encyclopaedia Judaica,* 2nd edition, edited by Michael Berenbaum and Fred Skolnik, 11:785–802. Detroit: Macmillan Reference USA, 2007.

Holt, P. M., Ann K. S. Lambton, and Bernard Lewis, eds. *The Central Islamic Lands.* Vol. 1 of *The Cambridge History of Islam.* Cambridge: Cambridge University Press, 1970.

Horowitz, Yehoshua, Menahem Ben-Sasson, Geoffrey Khan, Stefan C. Reif, and Stuart E. Rosenberg. "Genizah, Cairo." In *Encyclopaedia Judaica,* 2nd edition, edited by Michael Berenbaum and Fred Skolnik, 7:460–483. Detroit: Macmillan Reference USA, 2007.

Israel Broadcasting Authority. *HaToanim laKeter: Taalumot Keter Aram Tsova* (The Claimants to the Crown: The Mysteries of the Crown of Aleppo). Aired Apr. 1993.

JPS Hebrew-English Tanakh. Philadelphia: The Jewish Publication Society, 1999.

Johnson, Michael P. *All Honourable Men: The Social Origins of War in Lebanon.* London: Tauris, 2001.

Josephus, Flavius. *The War of the Jews.* In *The Works of Flavius Josephus*, translated by William Whiston. Leavitt and Allen, 1858.

Kahle, Paul E. *Masoreten des Westens*, vol. 1. Stuttgart: Kohlhammer, 1927.

———. "The new Hebrew Bible, Jerusalem 1953." Vetus Testamentum 3 (1953): 416–420.

———. *A Treatise on the Oldest Manuscripts of the Bible.* New York: Aldus, 1950.

Khoury, Philip S. *Syria and the French Mandate: The Politics of Arab Nationalism 1920–1945.* London: Tauris, 1987.

Kittel, Rudolf, Paul Kahle, et al., eds. *Biblia Hebraica.* Stuttgart: Privilegierte Wurttembergische Bibelanstalt, 1937.

Kohen, Arye. *HaAliyot haGedolot meArtsot haMizrah, Dape Meda uMivhar Mekorot: Suriya uLevanon (The Great Aliyot from the Countries of the East, Information and Selected Sources: Syria and Lebanon).* Ben Zvi Institute Series on Aliya from the East No. 4. Jerusalem: Ben Zvi Institute, 2000.

Kraus, Samuel. *"Bate Knesiot Atikim beErets Yisrael uveArtsot haKedem"* ("Ancient Synagogues in the Land of Israel and the Lands of the East"). In *Kovets haHevra haIvrit leHakirat Erets Yisrael veAtikoteha Mukdash leZekher Rav Avraham Moshe*

Lunts (Journal of the Hebrew Society for the Exploration of the Land of Israel Dedicated to the Memory of Abraham Moshe Luncz), edited by Isaiah Press and E. L. Sukenik, 221–249. Jerusalem: Darom, 1928.

Laniado, David. *LaKedoshim asher beErets [Aram Tsova]—LeToldot Hahme veRabane Erets (Haleb) (For the Holy Ones in Aleppo—The History of the Sages and Rabbis of Aleppo)*, 2nd ed. Jerusalem: Devash, 1980.

Laniado, Rafael Shlomo. *Roe Yisrael (The Shepherd of Israel)*, part 2. Jerusalem: N.p., 1904.

———. *Sheelot uTshuvot Kise Shlomo (The Seat of Solomon)*. Jerusalem: Zuckerman, 1900.

Laniado, Shmuel. *Dvash veHalav al Leshonekh: Sipure Kehilat Haleb veHahameha (Honey and Milk on the Tongue: Stories of the Aleppan Community and Its Sages)*. Jerusalem: N.p., 1998.

Lapidus, Ira Marvin. *Muslim Cities in the Later Middle Ages*. Cambridge: Harvard University Press, 1967.

Laqueur, Walter. *The History of Zionism*. New York: Tauris, 2003.

Levinger, D. S. *"Mekoriuto shel Ktav Yad Haleb"* ("The Authenticity of the Aleppo Manuscript"). In *Kitve Mifal haMikra shel haUniversita haIvrit (The Hebrew University Bible Project Series)*. Vol. 1: *Mehkarim beKeter Aram Tsova (Studies in the Crown of Aleppo)*, edited by Chaim Rabin, 38–65. Jerusalem: Magnes, 1968.

Lewis, Bernard. *The Jews of Islam*. Princeton, N.J.: Princeton University Press, 1984.

Luria, Benzion. *HaYehudim beSuriya Bime Shivat Tsion, haMishna vehaTalmud (The Jews in Syria during the Period of the Restoration, the Mishnah and the Talmud)*. Jerusalem: *HaHevra leHeker haMikra*, 1957.

Maggen, Michael. "Conservation of the Aleppo Codex." *Restaurator* 12 (1991): 116–130.

Maoz, Moshe. *Syria and Israel*. Oxford: Oxford University Press, 1995.

Minkoff, Harvey. "The Aleppo Codex: Ancient Bible from the Ashes." *Bible Review* 7 (Aug. 1991): 22–27, 38–40.

Morag, Shelomo. "Pronunciations of Hebrew." In *Encyclopaedia Judaica*, 2nd edition, edited by Michael Berenbaum and Fred Skolnik, 16:547–562. Detroit: Macmillan Reference USA, 2007.

Nehmad, Meir. *"Maamar Hakira al haKeter haYakar haNikra Keter Aram Tsova"* ("An Investigative Article on the Precious Codex Called the Crown of Aleppo"). Aleppo: MiDamesek, 1933.

Ofer, Yosef. "The History and Authority of the Aleppo Codex." In *The Jerusalem Crown Companion Volume,* edited by Mordechai Glatzer, 25–50. Jerusalem: Hebrew University Press, 2002.

———. "The Jerusalem Crown and Its Editorial Principles." In *The Jerusalem Crown Companion Volume,* edited by Mordechai Glatzer, 51–59. Jerusalem: Hebrew University Press, 2002.

———. *"Keta miSefer Shemot mehaHelek heHaser beKeter Aram Tsova"* ("A Fragment of Exodus from the Missing Parts of the Crown of Aleppo"). *Pe'amim* 41 (Autumn 1989): 41–48.

———. *"Keter Aram Tsova leOr Reshimotav shel M. D. Cassuto"* ("M. D. Cassuto's Notes on the Crown of Aleppo"). *Sefunot* 19 (1989): 277–344.

———. *"Keter Aram Tsova vehaTanakh shel Rav Shalom Shakhna Yelin"* ("The Aleppo Codex and the Bible of R. Shalom Shachna Yellin"). In *Sefer haYovel leRav Mordekhai Breuer (Rabbi Mordechai Breuer Festschrift: Collected Papers in Jewish Studies),* edited by M. Bar-Asher, 1:295–353. Jerusalem: Akademon, 1992.

———. "The Shattered Crown: The Aleppo Codex, 60 Years after the Riots." *Biblical Archeology Review* 34 (Sept.–Oct. 2008): 39–49.

Palestine Royal Commission Report, available at http://unispal.un.org/pdfs/ Cmd5479.pdf (accessed Oct. 15, 2009).

Penkower, Jordan S. "Maimonides and the Aleppo Codex." *Textus* 9 (Sept. 1981): 39–128.

———. *Nusah haTorah beKeter Aram Tsova — Edut Hadasha (New Evidence for the Pentateuch Text in the Crown of Aleppo).* Ramat Gan: Bar-Ilan University, 1992.

Pfeffer, Anshel. "Fragment of ancient parchment from Bible given to Jerusalem scholars." *Haaretz,* Nov. 7, 2007. Available at www.haaretz.com/hasen/ spages/920915.html (accessed Oct. 15, 2009).

Pipes, Daniel. *Greater Syria: The History of an Ambition.* New York: Oxford University Press, 1990.

Polachek, I., et al. "Fungi Not Fire Damaged Aleppo Codex." *Nature* 335 (Sept. 15, 1988): 203.

Porath, Zipporah. Letter, Nov. 30, 1947. Available at www.zionism-israel.com/ezine/Partition_A_Night_To_Remember.htm (accessed Oct. 20, 2009).

Rabin, Hayim. Interview of Murad Faham [Transcript]. 1976. Copy on file with the authors.

Roberts, Bleddyn J. *The Old Testament Text and Versions: The Hebrew Text in Transmission and the History of the Ancient Versions.* Cardiff: University of Wales Press, 1951.

Roth-Gerson, Leah. *The Jews of Syria as Reflected in the Greek Inscriptions.* (Jerusalem, 2001), esp. 262, s.v.: the inscription of Eli Bar-Natan (Heb.).

Russell, Alexander. *The Natural History of Aleppo.* 2nd ed. Vol. 2. London: Robinson, 1794.

Sanders, James A. "Understanding the Development of the Biblical Text." In *The Dead Sea Scrolls after Forty Years,* edited by Hershel Shanks et al., 57–71. Washington, D.C.: Biblical Archaeology Society, 1991.

Sapir, Yaakov. *Even Sapir.* Lyck, Prussia: 1866.

Sarna, Nahum M., Norman Henry Snaith, Leonard J. Greenspoon, Franklin T. Harkins, Angela Kim Harkins and Bernard Grossfeld. "Bible." In *Encyclopaedia Judaica,* 2nd edition, edited by Michael Berenbaum and Fred Skolnik, 3:572–679. Detroit: Macmillan Reference USA, 2007.

Schenhav, Dudu. *"HaKlaf veShimuro"* ("Parchment and Its Preservation"). *Ba-Muzeon* 1 (Mar. 1989): 18–19.

Schenhav, Dudu, Mikha Maggen, and Lea Ofer-Pandya. *"Keter Aram Tsova beMaabadot Muzeon Yisrael"* ("The Aleppo Codex in the Laboratories of the Israel Museum"). *Ba-Muzeon* 1 (Mar. 1989): 20–21.

Scholem, Gershom. *"Yediot Hadashot al Rav Yosef Ashkenazi"* ("New Information about Rabbi Yosef Ashkenazi"). *Tarbiz* 28 (1958): 59–89 and (1959): 201–235.

Schwarzfuchs, Simon R. "Crusades." In *Encyclopaedia Judaica,* 2nd edition, edited by Michael Berenbaum and Fred Skolnik, 5:310–315. Detroit: Macmillan Reference USA, 2007.

Segall, Joseph. *Travels through Northern Syria.* London: London Society for Promoting Christianity among the Jews, 1910.

Shamosh, Amnon. *"Arbaim Shana veArbaim Yom beIkvot haKeter"* ("Forty Years and Forty Days in Pursuit of the Crown"). In *Min haMaayan: Sihot uMaamarim (From the Well: Talks and Articles)*, 107–129. Jerusalem: Carta, 1988.

———. *HaKeter: Sipuro shel Keter Aram Tsova (The Crown: The Story of the Crown of Aleppo)*. Jerusalem: Hebrew University Press, 1987.

———. *Mishel Ezra Safra uBanav (Michel Ezra Safra and Sons)*. Ramat Gan: Givatayim, 1978.

Shtar Hekdesh (Writ of Consecration), Rabbinical Court, Jerusalem Region, Case No. 906/1962, May 23, 1962.

Sobernheim, M., and E. Mittwoch. *"Hebraische Inschriften in der Synagogue von Aleppo"* ("Hebrew Inscriptions in the Aleppo Synagogue"). In *Festschrift zum siebzigsten Geburtstage Jakob Guttmanns (Festschrift on the 70th Birthday of Jacob Guttmann)*, 273–285. Leipzig: Fock, 1915.

Stillman, Norman A. *The Jews of Arab Lands in Modern Times.* Philadelphia: The Jewish Publication Society, 1991.

Strack, Hermann. *A. Firkowitsch und seine Entdeckungen (Firkovitch and His Discoveries)*. Leipzig: N.p., 1876.

Sutton, David, and Isaac Kirzner, eds. *Aleppo: City of Scholars.* Brooklyn, N.Y.: Masorah, 2005.

Szyszman, Simon. *"La famille des massorètes karaïtes ben Asher et le Codex Alepensis"* ("The Karaite Ben-Asher Family of Masoretes and the Aleppo Codex"). *Revue Biblique* 73 (1966): 531–551.

Tawil, Moshe. Transcript of undated interview. Copy on file with the authors.

Wickes, William. *A Treatise on the Accentuation of the Twenty-One So-Called Prose Books of the Old Testament.* Oxford: Clarendon, 1877.

Würthwein, Ernst. *The Text of the Old Testament: An Introduction to the Biblia Hebraica,* translated by Erroll F. Rhodes. 2nd rev. ed. Grand Rapids, Mich.: Eerdmans, 1995.

Yeivin, Israel. *"Keter Aram Tsova, Nikudo veTeamav"* ("The Crown of Aleppo: Its Vocalization and Accentuation"). In *Kitve Mifal haMikra shel haUniversita haIvrit (The Hebrew University Bible Project Series)*. Vol. 3: *Mehkarim beKeter Aram Tsova (Studies in the Crown of Aleppo)*, edited by Moshe Goshen-Gottstein. Jerusalem: Hebrew University Press, 1968.

Zenner, Walter P. *A Global Community: The Jews from Aleppo, Syria.* Detroit: Wayne State University Press, 2000.

———. *"HaHayim haPnimiyim shel Yehude Suriya beShelhe haTkufa haOtomanit"* ("The Internal Life of Syrian Jewry at the End of the Ottoman Period"). *Pe'amim* (Autumn 1979): 45–58.

———. "Jews in Late Ottoman Syria: Community, Family and Religion." In *Jewish Societies in the Middle East: Community, Culture and Authority*, edited by Shlomo Deshen and Walter P. Zenner, 187–209. Lanham, Md.: University Press of America, 1982.

———. "Jews in Late Ottoman Syria: External Relations." In *Jewish Societies in the Middle East: Community, Culture and Authority*, edited by Shlomo Deshen and Walter P. Zenner, 155–186. Lanham, Md.: University Press of America, 1982.

———. "Syrian Jews and Their Non-Jewish Neighbors in Late Ottoman Times." In *Jews Among Muslims: Communities in the Precolonial Middle East*, edited by Shlomo Deshen and Walter P. Zenner, 161–186. New York: New York University Press, 1996.

Zer, Rafael Yitzhak. *"HeHaya Masran haKeter Rabani o Karai?"* ("Was the Masorete of the Crown of Aleppo a Rabbanite or a Karaite?") *Sefunot* 23 (2003): 573–587.

———. *"Meorot Natan leRabi Yaakov Sapir"* ("R. Ya'aqov Sappir's *Meoroth Nathan*"). Lešonénu 50 (1986): 151–213.

Zohar, Zvi. "And Art Scroll Created Aleppo in Its Own Image." In *Aleppan Jewry*, edited by Miriam Frenkel et al., in press.

———. *Drama Hevratit-Tarbutit beHaleb haMandatorit (A Social-Cultural Drama in Mandatory Aleppo)*. Jerusalem: Hebrew University Press, 2003.

———. *"Shamranut Lohemet: Kavim leManhigutam haHevratit-Datit shel Hahme Haleb baEt haHadasha"* ("Fighting Conservatism: Characteristics of the Social-Religious Leadership of the Sages of Aleppo in the Modern Era"). *Pe'amim* 55 (1993): 57–78.

Zucker, Moshe M. *"Neged Mi Katav Rav Saadia Gaon et haPiyut 'Esa Meshali'?"* ("Against Whom Did Saadiah Gaon Write His Piyut 'Esa Meshali'?"). *Tarbiz* 27 (1957–58): 61–82.

Internet Resources

Aleppo Codex. www.aleppocodex.org.
Ben-Zvi Institute. www.ybz.org.il (in Hebrew).

Page numbers in *italics* indicate illustrations
Page numbers in **bold** indicate glossary entries
Page numbers for tables are noted by the letter "t"
Center insert indicates color illustrations located in the center of the book

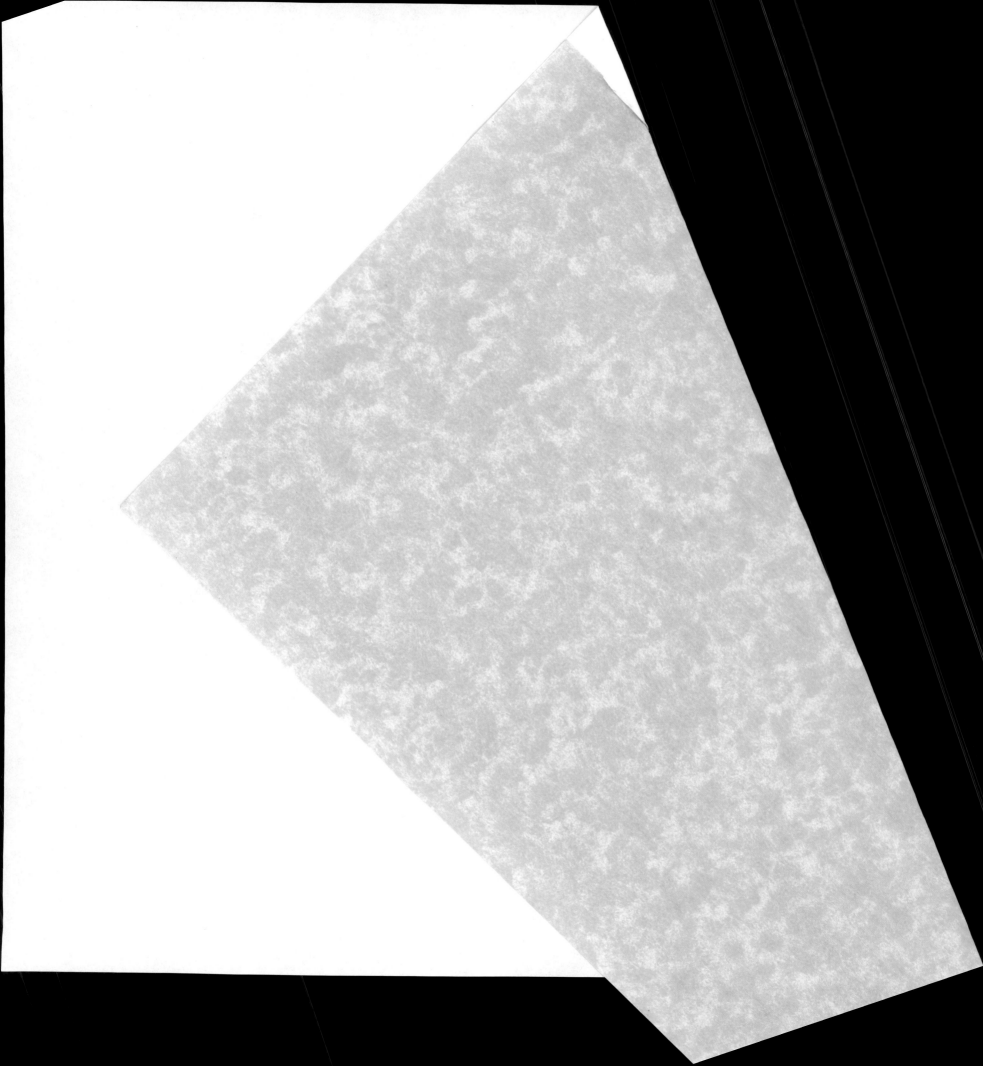